LA 217 .#46

Also by Nat Hentoff

DOES ANYBODY GIVE A DAMN?

Nat Hento

DOES
ANYBODY
GIVE
A DAMN?

n Education

Alfred A. Knopf   New York   1977

THIS IS A BORZOI BOOK
PUBLISHED BY ALFRED A. KNOPF, INC.

Copyright © 1977 by Namar Productions, Ltd.

Library of Congress Cataloging in Publication Data

Hentoff, Nat.
  Does anybody give a damn?

  1. Education—United States. I. Title.
LA217.H46 1977 370'.973 76-47611
ISBN 0-394-40933-7

Manufactured in the United States of America

FIRST EDITION

For Dr. Kenneth Bancroft Clark

ACKNOWLEDGMENTS

I am grateful to the John Simon Guggenheim Memorial Foundation for the fellowship that made it possible for me to do part of the research for this book. Some of the other sections were originally written, in different form, for *The New Yorker*, and I am also grateful to its editor, William Shawn.

I am particularly indebted to George Dennison and the late Paul Goodman, both exemplary teachers of learning.

CONTENTS

DOES ANYBODY GIVE A DAMN?

Introduction

Miss Keyes, the principal of the William Lloyd Garrison Elementary School in the Roxbury section of Boston, was a tall, ample, elderly, authoritarian, Victorian-looking woman who held her teachers strictly accountable. The teachers in turn held each of us accountable. They had no doubt that we were capable of learning. All of us were white, practically all of us were Jewish, and the teachers—most of whom were Irish—never thought of not accepting the folk wisdom that Jews were smart. So they allowed us no excuses, no backsliding. And we were smart.

On graduation, I went off to Boston Latin School, also a public school but entered only through competitive examination. There my peers were more heterogeneous (there was even one black youngster in my class); and all of us, as had been the case at Latin School since the seventeenth century, were expected to learn a great deal. And so we did.

The teachers at Boston Latin School would have agreed with the precept of Dr. Kenneth Clark: "Any theory that a child shouldn't be pressured, that he shouldn't be 'frustrated,' imposes on the child the most horrible form of self-depreciation.

The essential ingredient in teaching children is to respect the child by *insisting* that he does learn."

My experience as a public school student took place in the 1930s. The schools of Boston did for me what my parents intended they should do. Indeed, my parents could have conceived no other outcome. Neither of them, both Russian immigrants, had gone to college; but their American son would. And having been prepared by the public schools, their American son did.

It wasn't until the early 1960s that I again gave any sustained thought to elementary and secondary schooling. I had been a writer on jazz and then ineluctably on civil rights (black music coming from black people). Absorption in civil rights led, also inescapably, to a focus on such urban survival matters as jobs, housing, health services, and the courts. It eventually occurred to me—I was a slow learner in some respects—that the most fundamental urban beat of all was education. For blacks, Puerto Ricans, Chicanos, and the rest of the "disadvantaged" (the passive euphemism of the time for those discriminated against), the schools, after all, were supposed to be the primary way up, just as they had been for my family.

At one of the first New York City Board of Education meetings I went to, a black father got up to speak. He had been a school dropout in the South, I learned later, came north, worked at a string of menial jobs, and eventually wound up in a dead-end factory slot which paid him some ninety dollars a week. His hope was his child, and he had watched her fall farther and farther behind each year of school.

The black father was very angry. "You people," he said to the board, "operate a goddamn monopoly, like the telephone company. I got no choice where I send my child to school. I can only send her where it's free. And she's not learning. Damn it, that's *your* responsibility, it's the principal's responsibility, it's the teacher's responsibility that she's not learning."

The more or less distinguished members of the Board of Education looked on impassively.

"When you fail, when everybody fails my child"—the father's voice had gotten thick with rage and no little grief—"what happens? Nothing. Nobody gets fired. Nothing happens to nobody except my child."

He sat down, the meeting went on, and for the rest of the night, no member of the Board of Education referred to what he had said.

A few years later, reporting on the same kind of parent anger in his book *The Airtight Cage* (about the poor on Manhattan's Upper West Side), Joseph Lyford pointed out another dimension of the schools' failure. He quoted a guidance counselor at a public school who noted that black and Hispanic parents, just like white parents, had

> tremendous ambition for their children to do well in school. ... The child is painfully aware of the parents' anxiety, which works great hardships both ways. As the child begins to fall behind, the parent becomes more and more anxious and friction develops. By the time the child is nine or ten and the parents see that, despite all their desire, the child is not going to make it, they feel a personal humiliation. They really take it out on the child, which only drives the child down deeper.

Why were the schools failing these children and their parents? In some cases—in New York and other cities whose schools I have explored—the answer is a matter of attitude. There are teachers, principals, school board members, and budget-determining legislators who agree with William O'Connor, a former chairman of the Boston School Committee: "We have no inferior education in our schools. What we have been getting is an inferior type of student."

Call it racism, or class bias, or plain realism, or whatever you will, this is also the conviction that certain kinds of children from certain kinds of backgrounds can learn only a certain amount. The school cannot be expected to make up for the multi-disciplinary deprivation which has already shaped, or twisted, these children before they ever started school and which continues to sap whatever capabilities they have while they are attending school. Little if any intellectual stimulation at home; broken families; violent families and mean streets. The school can try to civilize these kids, some of them anyway, but they *are* an inferior type of student. Those who refuse to admit this aren't doing these children any good because they are setting expectations for them that they cannot possibly fulfill. This point of view is very widespread indeed, though almost never any longer expressed aloud by whites, except when alone with each other.

There is another attitude, also widespread, which still gingerly holds to the notion that *any* child can be successfully taught—if only one knew how. Dr. Nathan Brown, a diligent, conscientious educator who at one time was acting superintendent of schools in New York City, used to insist that a great deal more research was needed to find out why the children of the poor "are not profiting from the educational program. . . . Money is being spent on new gimmicks, but nobody knows the cause-and-effect relationship. . . . We have offered all kinds of solutions, but they are not producing results and nobody knows why."

Of course, not only the children of the poor "are not profiting from the educational program," although a dismayingly disproportionate percentage of them are among the casualties of schooling. In testimony before the Senate Subcommittee on Juvenile Delinquency in April 1975, James A. Harris, then president of the National Education Association, noted that 23 percent of *all* schoolchildren are failing to graduate. Another large segment of failures does graduate, but as functional illiterates. Surely not all those kids are poor.

Mr. Harris did not explain exactly why the schools, with all the marvels of modern pedagogy, are foundering, but he did emphasize quite reasonably that "If 23 percent of anything else failed—23 percent of the automobiles did not run, 23 percent of the buildings fell down, 23 percent of stuffed ham spoiled— we'd look at the producer. The schools, here, are not blameless."

The extent, however, to which the schools rather than the students are basically culpable is an exceedingly sensitive point with most of those who run and teach in these institutions. They are professionals—a point they underline whenever, for example, there is any question of lay people, such as parents, becoming involved in helping set standards of school performance and accountability. Only professional educators, after all, are qualified to evaluate professional educators. Just as only doctors can evaluate medical treatment.

But, some bewildered and exacerbated parents say, apart from the fact that doctors themselves seldom do hold any of their colleagues accountable for culpable medical failures, a lay citizen can change doctors if he is dissatisfied—and still alive. The parent of a schoolchild, unless he has the money for private or parochial education, is subject to an educational monopoly. The public schools *are* like the telephone company.

It is to the public school systems that 90 percent of the kids in this country are sent for their compulsory schooling, and that's where they are sorted out, including in their own heads, for the future. That's where some learn confidence in themselves and others learn they are dumb and thereby headed for a life somewhere down there below.

As for the occasionally modish arguments to the effect that schooling really doesn't make much of a difference, it is instructive that all who make such arguments—and have the capacity to ensure their wide dissemination—are themselves well schooled. The teen-age dropout or pushout, if you will, knows better. Particularly if he is poor. He has been deschooled. But what next?

What follows in this book, however, is not yet another bill of indictment against the one big educational telephone company. My main interest all along in writing about education has been in finding ways in which certain schools can and do work for all kids, or for a larger percentage of them than is or has been the norm. But I also look for schools, principals, and teachers whose ways of enabling even the most "uneducable" kids to learn are not so *sui generis* that they can't take root anywhere else. In the jargon of applications for foundation grants, everything you read in this book is "replicable."

This book is neither apocalyptic nor despairing. It is a report of a continuing battle by quite diverse people, kids and adults, against the school odds. To me, some of them are rather heroic, in wholly unexpected ways; but in any case, they are stubbornly non-abstract. And what they have discovered—about learning, about themselves—can be made real for all kinds of children. Ghetto kids are not the only ones whose lives—far beyond childhood—are blighted by what happens and does not happen to them in school.

The reader, in taking these journeys, is entitled to know what my own approach to learning is. I would describe it as ecumenically pragmatic. Through more than a decade of writing on schools, I have become cautious about all labels placed on what is proclaimed as "more effective" education—open classrooms and corridors, "getting back to basics," alternative learning settings outside the system, alternatives within the system, "affective" learning, et al. What I keep searching for are schools where children really do learn—whatever labels the schools or principals or teachers have attached to how this happens.

In the early 1960s, while researching my first book on education, *Our Children Are Dying,* I learned a lasting lesson in writing about learning. The book was about a central Harlem school of which Dr. Elliott Shapiro (who returns in this book) was the principal. There, each teacher was free to work in his own way—provided that he was not just a custodian or a time-server. Accordingly, one second-grade class was conducted by a teacher who, when he felt it necessary, was as much therapist as instructor. Children often came to him with problems that had nothing to do with math or spelling—problems at home, problems in the street and the schoolyard. He listened and advised and visited the children's homes and was always available for a kid who needed an adult who could be trusted. Occasionally I would walk into his room and see him hugging a sobbing child. This teacher agreed with George Dennison, author of *The Lives of Children,* that "the business of a school is not, or should not be, mere instruction, but the life of the child." And the problems in the life of a child do, of course, greatly impinge on schoolwork. If the former seem insoluble, there is hardly any concentration left for the latter. Yet this teacher, for all his involvement in the children's non-school predicaments, was also much concerned with academics, and eventually most of his kids did learn.

On the other hand, there was a fifth-grade teacher who first appeared unyieldingly stern directing his tightly disciplined classroom in the manner and tone of a drill sergeant. Initially I took notes in his cold class in the form of a denunciation-to-come; but as the months went by, it became unexpectedly clear to me that the kids in his room not only were industriously doing the sizable amount of work he required of them, but were also eager to push on. He quite powerfully communicated to them his insistent confidence that they *could* learn, and as the children responded to his expectations of them, they began to enjoy a rising sense of themselves as capable learners and wanted to keep heightening that sense.

This teacher, I should add, worked harder than all but perhaps five or six other teachers I have observed over the years. Not only in class, where he was continually on top of everything that was going on and knew the strengths and deficiencies of each child with great specificity, but also after school and on weekends, which he devoted to carefully grading papers and devising new exercises with which he could quicken his students' skills. "I make them *strain* so that they can experience success," he told me, "and that success experience makes them work harder. Once the child gets that satisfaction, he'll work no matter what's happening at home."

I could hardly continue feeling censorious about his teaching style, authoritarian though it was, because he was so obviously awakening the children he taught to their potential. And that's when I stopped going automatically by labels and styles. I do remain critical of many other authoritarian teachers, however, because they teach subjects, not children. Every lesson for every day in the school year is fully planned, and the teacher moves unswervingly from one lesson to the next. The kids keep up as best they can, and those who fall behind are left to meditate on their irredeemable dumbness.

Yet teachers with more "open" styles also vary markedly. Some are so intent on cultivating the children's *feelings* that they fear making too many intellectual demands on a kid lest he "lose touch," as they say, with his feelings and become "too competitive." With that kind of benign intellectual neglect, he may also become pretty dumb while his feelings exfoliate. Then there are teachers who have chosen non-traditional ways of teaching because they strongly believe that many children do move more genuinely into learning if they have choices of what they want to learn at any given time of day rather than being forced to keep up with what everyone else is studying according to a teacher's fixed schedule. But the most valuable of these teachers are not afraid of making demands on kids in an "open" classroom. They keep detailed logs of how each child is progressing in all the basic skills—and how well he *should* be doing in relation to his capacities. They recognize that one of the keenest feelings, however ambivalent, in childhood is wanting to grow up; and one definition of growing up absurd is growing up ignorant.

This book about schools where kids don't turn absurd encompasses widely different approaches to enabling youngsters to grow up intelligent, and to *know* that they're intelligent, despite what they may have been told previously in school. There are diverse approaches as well to other matters of educational policy and practice. Kids are given all sorts of tests, for instance, but what about continued evaluation of teachers and administrators? A corollary motif is the politics of education. Who controls the schools? Who prevents their being made accountable for their failures? And is that control immutable?

There is also a learning issue I consider so important that it provides this book with its first chapter—the question of why schoolchildren are the only Americans who can be legally, officially beaten. I begin with corporal punishment because a primary reason for its sturdy survival in the schools is the insistence by a majority of teachers and school administrators throughout the country that if the right to hit kids were taken away from them, they would be less "effective" educators. This quite passionately held position of so many professional educators reveals an attitude toward teaching and toward the young that should chill every parent with a child in school and, for that matter, any adult who considers himself reasonably humane.

But there is no mass outrage against the beating of schoolchildren as part of the learning experience. After all, little has been written about the extent, and the effects, of corporal punishment in the 80 percent of American schools that permit it. And that is why we begin at this most primitive level of schooling in these United States.

Does Eric Sevareid's Kid Get Hit in School?

In 1973, Russell Carl Baker, a sixth-grader in the small textile town of Gibsonville, North Carolina, was playing ball in school. At the time, he was not supposed to be playing ball; and to instruct him memorably in this rule of school law, Russell Baker's teacher took a wooden drawer divider (about two inches wide, thirteen inches long, and three-eighths of an inch thick) and whacked the boy thrice in front of the class. It happened to be a social studies class.

In Gibsonville, as in most schools throughout the country, corporal punishment is a venerable learning device. Russell Baker's mother, however, had explicitly informed school authorities, long before her son's criminal act of ballplaying, that she did not want her son hit—ever—because of his frailty and because such punishment, she was convinced, violated her right to "familial privacy."

Accordingly, Virginia Baker brought suit, claiming that the North Carolina law permitting corporal punishment was unconstitutional. In addition to the "familial privacy" argument, she maintained that her son had been whacked without due process and that the punishment had been arbitrary and applied with excessive force. The case moved through the courts, eventually reaching a three-judge federal panel which held that a state can allow teachers and other school personnel to hit a child—even when a parent objects.

The three-judge court did set up three qualifying "safeguards," all of which can easily be subverted by school officials: (1) corporal punishment should not be the "first line" of punishment, and children should be told in advance what kinds of misbehavior will lead to their getting belted; (2) a second teacher should witness the punishment; and (3) those parents requesting a written explanation of the punishment can get it —presumably suitable for framing.

Virginia Baker appealed that ruling, and on October 20, 1975, the United States Supreme Court, without issuing an opinion of its own, upheld the decision of the lower court. The high court thereby affirmed the constitutionality of corporal punishment in the particular case of the unfortunate Russell Baker; but since the Supreme Court refrained from giving its reasoning, it is still possible that another case, with a different set of circumstances, might cause the justices to take a contrary view of corporal punishment. Another possibility of relief, of course, is that a differently composed Supreme Court, years hence, might decide otherwise.

Nonetheless, the high court's support, in 1975, of the assaulting of a sixth-grade boy with a heavy piece of wood was, as *The New York Times* observed editorially, "an extraordinarily regressive ruling." As for those "safeguards" devised by the lower court to assure the "fairness" of corporal punishment, the *Times* observed: "Too vague to prevent serious abuses, these restrictions tell more about judicial confusion than about the future course of school discipline."

Not only the judiciary is confused, however, on the matter of legally beating schoolchildren. Shortly after the Supreme Court's action, Eric Sevareid, CBS-TV's resident moral philosopher, spoke for a substantial majority of the citizenry—judging by Gallup and other polls of public attitudes toward corporal punishment—when he jocularly began one of his commentaries by saying, "How kid-whacking got to be a constitutional question, we haven't the faintest idea." To be sure, Sevareid added, there are those who claim that hitting schoolchildren is dehumanizing. But certainly adults with a sense of proportion know that kid-whacking, Sevareid emphasized, "is civilizing."

Watching Sevareid, I thought of the kids I have talked to in various parts of the country who have been intensively "civilized" by violent adults in the public schools. Some of this kid-whacking, as Sevareid calls it, has been more psychically than physically wounding. Some—as court cases below will indicate—has been just plain brutal. And some has been of a quite special order of cruelty. A few years ago, for example, I spoke to the parents of a ten-year-old boy in a small Texas town who was dying of a blood disease. The school knew he was dying, but the kid was whacked anyway, and whacked hard, for talking in class. It happened more than once.

"I have given up trying to understand how people could do that," the father said to me once, "people who say they're educators. They have a sickness that is beyond me. But what still makes me furious is that there wasn't a damn thing I could do about it. They told me they had the right to beat my boy. And there it was, right in the law." His parents, after the boy died, gave me a picture of him, which I kept for some months until I could no longer bear keeping it.

Soon after I had talked with that father, I spent a Saturday afternoon with a group of youngsters in North Dallas. Mostly white, they ranged from seven-year-olds to kids attending junior high school. We all sat around a table in the library of a Unitarian church, and as they spoke of the routinely pervasive use of force against them in the Dallas schools, I was at first startled, and then dismayed, by the lack of indignation—except in a few of the older kids—as they told of what had been done to them. A rebel teacher said to me later, "By now, they think getting hit, no matter how slight the infraction, is normal. They have been successfully beaten down."

At the library table, the youngsters were politely trying to instruct me in the ecology of violence in their schools.

"When I was in the fourth grade," one youngster said matter-of-factly, "you'd get an extra lick if you moved or if you cried out while you were getting hit. Well, it was kind of hard not to move when you were being hit with a two-by-four. The paddle had holes in it besides. That makes it hurt more."

"What did you get hit for?" I asked the boy.

"Being late. For every minute you were late to class, you'd get a lick."

The other children nodded. They had had similar experiences.

"I was chewing gum," a girl with long blond hair told me, "and they used three paddles on me. The first two broke. Some of those teachers are really hitting freaks. Where my little brother goes—he's in fifth grade—by the end of the first week of school last month, the teacher had given licks to everybody in that class."

"Why?" I asked, already having heard something of that teacher from a Dallas parent.

"Oh, they were kind of noisy, you know."

"Have you heard about 'double-stamp day'?" A thin, dark-haired boy spoke up. I told him I had seen the term in a story in the *Dallas Morning News* about a junior high school.

"Yeah," he said. "That's Stockard. I go there. Last year, one of the teachers had a 'double-stamp day' on Wednesdays. You'd get double the number of licks for everything you did wrong that day. Like having your shirttails out or forgetting to say 'Sir.' He's a mean one."

"How about the principal in North Dallas?" a teen-ager said. "The one with the paddle that has his name on it: 'Elmer the Terrible.' My little cousin goes there. The principal's got that paddle with him all the time—walking around the halls, going into classrooms asking the teacher if everything's under control. Last week the bastard even showed up in the playground with it. Christ, you're supposed to be able to make some noise in the playground! My cousin, he's scared to go to school. He ain't been hit yet, but he figures that, sooner or later, Elmer the Terrible's going to get him."

Appropriately, in this city of Elmer the Terrible, the National Committee to Abolish Corporal Punishment in the Schools was founded, in October 1972, as an outgrowth of a national conference on corporal punishment held in May 1972 in New York under the auspices of the American Civil Liberties Union and the American Orthopsychiatric Association. The follow-up group, of which I was and am a member, consists of teachers, lawyers, parents, students, psychologists, and writers from various parts of the country. We chose Dallas as the natal place of our committee because at the time it was clearly the corporal punishment capital of the nation. (From November 1971 to May 1972, according to official Dallas school statistics, there had been *reported* applications of physical punishment to 24,305 children. Total enrollment in the Dallas Independent School District during that period was 166,353.)

The beat still goes on in the Dallas schools, but it is no longer possible to be at all precise concerning the incidence of corporal punishment in that city since school officials now guard these statistics closely. In any case, whether or not Dallas remains the kid-whacking center of the nation, the attitudes of its school officials and teachers continue to parallel those of their counterparts in the majority of school districts around the country. They fervently believe, as Dallas school superintendent Dr. Nolan Estes puts it, that "until there is a Utopian society," paddling and other violence against children is essential in classrooms as "a last resort." Dr. Estes, moreover, is sternly on record as pledging that he would not serve as head of any school system in which corporal punishment is prohibited.

Elsewhere in the country, corporal punishment in public schools is barred by law in only two states (New Jersey and Massachusetts) and in all but a number of rural counties in a third (Maryland). It has also been abolished in some city school systems, among them New York, Baltimore, Chicago, and Grosse Pointe, Michigan.

In many school systems, however, an observation made in 1853 by the Indiana Supreme Court (*Cooper* v. *McJunkin*) still holds:

> The public seems to cling to the despotism in the government of schools which has been discarded everywhere else. . . . The husband can no longer moderately chastise his wife; nor . . . the master his servant or his apprentice. Even the degrading cruelties of the naval service have been arrested. Why the person of the schoolboy . . . should be less sacred in the eyes of the law than that of the apprentice or the sailor, is not easily explained.

"Sacred!" a former high school teacher in Wheelersburg, Ohio, hooted when shown that 1853 opinion. "Where I taught, any teacher may still paddle any student for any reason. And there are several male teachers, proudly and threateningly bearing their foot-long wooden paddles, who often stand in the halls during the changing of classes as an inspiration, I suppose, to the students."

A minister in Illinois has told me of his daughter, "a bright and socially at ease six-year-old" who "looked forward to attending kindergarten with great joy, and even anticipated attending first grade this year with considerable enthusiasm. In each instance, however, her enthusiasm has been quickly dampened by the repeated warnings of physical punishment—specifically, the application of a paddle, which her teachers keep for 'disciplinary' reasons. Although she herself has never been punished (despite an occasional threat to do so if she didn't stop crying about the threat to do so), its use on others makes the threat convincing and has caused irreparable damage to her attitude toward school, teachers, and education generally."

"Irreparable" is a premature judgment, I hope, but it is not difficult to understand why this child's enthusiasm for school has decidedly diminished.

A social studies teacher in San Pedro, California, has reported the case of a seventeen-year-old senior who had missed a meeting of the football team. An assistant coach gave the student the choice of turning in his football uniform or getting what is referred to in that school as a "swat." The young man took the latter option because he wanted to finish the football season. After the assistant coach had administered the swat, he declared, with professional pride, "I lifted him off the floor."

Alan Button, author of *The Authentic Child* and a member of the Department of Psychology at Fresno State College, California, has collected a number of corporal punishment case histories in the public schools of Fresno. This is one of them:

Don, nine. IQ: 133. Repeating third grade, having received solid F's first time around. His teacher, whom I consider an anxiety hysteric, ineffectual, and prone to weeping in class, would send him almost daily to the principal's office for "smart talk" and questioning her authority. (The boy corrected her mispronunciation of the river Thames in class one day—"That's pronounced 'Temz,' Miss X"—and was sent to the principal for spanking for insubordination.) Developed school phobias, nightmares, and night terrors in third grade, began torturing family cat. Seemed to me to be a direct function of consistent spanking at school, together with lack of support from his own family, who took the position that the teachers and principals were right and that they, his family, shouldn't interfere. Is flunking the third grade this year, too.

A customary explanation by those who insist on the continued need for corporal punishment is that of Dr. Nolan Estes: "We often have to use negative reinforcement to help the child learn self-discipline." Or as Albert Fondy, president of the Pittsburgh Teachers Federation, has put it, "Until somebody comes up with an alternative, we'll support it [corporal punishment]. It's a quick way to show disapproval—like the city giving me a ticket when I park illegally."

A youngster in the Pittsburgh schools questions Mr. Fondy's analogy. "When he parks illegally," the boy said to me, "Fondy doesn't get *hit* by the cop."

Mr. Fondy and the forces he heads in that city exemplify the tenacity of true believers in corporal punishment. Since 1970, an anti–corporal punishment coalition of Pittsburgh citizens has persuaded the school board to phase out the official hitting of kids, but on five separate occasions, the Pittsburgh Teachers Federation has insisted that a clause be put into a new contract mandating that the school board reconsider the abolition of corporal punishment. One particularly bitter eight-week strike, in the winter of 1975–76, finally approached settlement on money terms but was almost prolonged by teachers insisting they be given, by contract, the undisputed right to whack kids. They finally settled when it was agreed that the school board would once again vote on the restoration of corporal punishment.

I interviewed teachers' union president Albert Fondy during an earlier round of contract negotiations and suggested he look into studies on the harmful effects of corporal punishment by such researchers as Dr. David Gil, a professor of social policy at Brandeis University. (In his book *Violence Against Children,* as in his testimony in various courts in support of suits seeking to abolish corporal punishment, Dr. Gil relates physical abuse of schoolchildren to "culturally sanctioned individual acts of violence against children within the family." Dr. Gil is working for legislation to end corporal punishment in schools and in all other institutions dealing with children—both to protect young people and also because "such legislation is ... likely to affect child-rearing attitudes and practices in American homes, for it would symbolize society's growing rejection of violence against children." In addition, Dr. Gil points out that wherever it takes place, "Rarely, if ever, is corporal punishment administered for the benefit of the attacked child. . . . Usually it serves the immediate needs of the attacking adult who is seeking relief from his uncontrollable anger and stress.")

The president of the Pittsburgh Teachers Federation did not appear likely to accept my suggestion that he examine the research on violence against children. "Look," he told me. "It's simple. The members of my union want to keep corporal punishment as an option in case they need it for discipline. So long as the teachers want it, I'm not going to oppose it. Besides, I was hit as a kid in school, and it didn't do me any harm."

Pittsburgh's teachers are not at all unique in their ardent desire to hold on to violence as an option for dealing with children. A 1969 poll by the National Education Association Research Division indicated that 65.7 percent of teachers favored the infliction of physical pain when necessary—a decline from the 71.6 percent who shared that view in 1960, but nonetheless a solid majority. The decline, however, is somewhat encouraging, perhaps indicating that younger members of the profession are more resourceful in their ways of dealing with actual and potential disciplinary problems.

Nonetheless, in Cleveland, where corporal punishment is both legal and often used, that city's teachers made their prohitting convictions clear a few years ago when a mother filed suit charging that her son had been paddled against her wishes. James O'Meara, president of the Cleveland Teachers Union, said that his members were "really hot" on the issue and intended to "fight to keep" their authority to paddle.

Most teachers in Dallas remain decidedly of the same view. A Washington official of the National Education Association, with which the majority of Dallas's organized teachers are affiliated, says, with some pain about her colleagues in that city, "They're not even embarrassed about their stand." (An N.E.A. task force report on corporal punishment, published in 1972, opposes its use; but many of the N.E.A.'s more than 1,700,000 members throughout the country have yet to agree with the task force's recommendation that physical punishment be eliminated as a means of maintaining discipline in the schools. "We published the report, all right," an N.E.A. official told me in 1976, "but I don't think it's had much effect.")

Nor are many of the country's principals and other school administrators disturbed by the fact that in America, "the degrading cruelties of the naval service" remain only in the schools. By contrast, corporal punishment in schools has been banned in the Netherlands (1850), France (1887), Finland (1890), Sweden (1958), and Denmark (1968). In 1783, Poland, influenced by John Locke's "Some Thoughts on Education," abolished corporal punishment, which is also prohibited now in the Soviet Union and all other communist bloc countries. Yet in May 1971, *Nation's Schools* surveyed 13,000 school administrators in the fifty states. Of the 62 percent responding, 74 percent said that corporal punishment is applied in their districts, and 64 percent answered affirmatively the question: "Do you feel that corporal punishment has proved itself to be an effective instrument in assuring discipline?"

Said one superintendent, with what must have seemed to him unassailable reasonableness, "A student has the choice of cooperation and the teacher the choice of punishment."

In a more recent survey of school administrators, published in the June 1974 issue of *Phi Delta Kappa,* a monthly journal of education, seventy of the country's largest school districts were asked whether corporal punishment was practiced in their schools. Of the fifty replying, 80 percent acknowledged, with no discernible discomfort, that they practice kidwhacking.

In the minority is Kenton E. Stephens, superintendent of schools in Oak Park, Illinois. In September 1970, he instructed all teachers and supervisors to stop hitting students; and in August 1972, in one of his regular bulletins to all employees in the district, Superintendent Stephens reminded them not "to take refuge in a technique which demeans both student and teacher."

From what I have discovered, visiting many other schools in the country, Kenton Stephens's position is regarded as eccentric, let alone foolish, by most of his colleagues.

My interest in kid-whacking began in 1971 when, on invitation from the American Civil Liberties Union, I researched and wrote a report on the state of students' rights in the nation's schools. In 1969, the Supreme Court had declared (*Tinker* v. *Des Moines Independent Community School District*) that students are "persons" under the Constitution and thereby have fundamental rights and liberties which school authorities are required to respect. Two years before, the Court had held (*in re Gault*) that "neither the Fourteenth Amendment nor the Bill of Rights is for adults alone." And back in 1943, the Supreme Court had emphasized (*West Virginia Board of Education* v. *Barnette*) that "educating the young for citizenship is reason for scrupulous protection of Constitutional freedoms of the individual, if we are not to strangle the free mind at its source and teach youth to discount important principles of our government as mere platitudes."

In my travels around the country, then and since, I found that these Supreme Court decisions had not markedly affected the attitudes and actions of many teachers and supervisors. Students, for example, still have to fight for their First Amendment right to publish in districts in which principals routinely exercise prior restraint over the school newspaper. In some schools, although there is no censorship, sanctions are exercised against certain students who have used their First Amendment rights. A high school principal in South Carolina, for example, removed a student's name from the ballot for a school election because the boy had criticized the school administration in the school paper.

"But that's unconstitutional!" the stubbornly libertarian student said.

"The constitution of this school," his principal instructed him, "takes precedence over the United States Constitution."

I also found many instances of students being summarily tossed out of school (suspended or expelled) as part of their learning process. (In 1975, the Supreme Court, in *Goss* v. *Lopez* and *Wood* v. *Strickland,* finally set minimal due process safeguards for such cases, including the possibility of money damages against school officials who violate those safeguards. The decisions are useful precedents, but the protections are slight, and abuses continue.) In addition, as I visited schools in various states, I came across a sizable number of cases in which supposedly private records of students—including comments about them by teachers, guidance counselors, and school psychologists—were being released, without the students or their families knowing it, to all kinds of unauthorized inquirers, from police to prospective employers. (This release of school records without parental approval is now prohibited by federal law, but there is no monitoring system to assure that school administrators obey this law. Its implementation depends entirely on the vigilance of parents. And so abuses in this area also continue.)

What most astonished me, however, in researching that A.C.L.U. report, was the extent to which corporal punishment flourishes in the public schools.

I had not given the phenomenon much thought since my own elementary school years in Boston. At the William Lloyd Garrison Elementary School, to be sure, one of us, on occasion, would leave the classroom to be led to judgment. In the principal's office, the offending child would extend a hand, palm up, and be administered, depending on his crime, a certain number of whacks with a rattan switch. At the time, the rattan was a fact of childhood life, like the weather. We did not reflect much on the possibility of changing either.

By the time I started writing about education, in the 1960s, I assumed at first that the rattan, and other such atavistic teaching "tools," had disappeared not only at the William Lloyd Garrison School but also at nearly all others. Oh, in some rural fastnesses somewhere in the country there might still be a hitting teacher; but surely, everywhere else teachers would no more hit kids than teach them the world is flat. This must be so, I thought, because in all the books on education proliferating in the '60s—including those heralding radical transformations of the schools—there was hardly a mention of corporal punishment. It had to be obsolete. For that matter, in the books on schools of the 1970s, the physical punishment of children is also hardly ever mentioned.

It took me a while, therefore, to become convinced that the battering of schoolchildren is as commonplace as the evidence I gathered continued to show. But that evidence kept on piling up.

Like a guidance (*sic*) counselor in eastern rural New York State who stoutly informed Richard Gummere, Jr., a Columbia University official, that he regularly knocks youngsters to the floor of his office "to improve the school's morale."

Or this contribution to learning theory by a Los Angeles math teacher, as recalled by one of his sixth-grade students: "It was ten minutes to three. I was doing math drills in front of the class, and I kept getting mixed up, so the teacher made me put my right hand on the desk. Every time I said the wrong number, he whacked my hand with the side of his ruler. At three-fifteen I still couldn't get the answers right and my hand was swollen and purple."

A few years ago, I learned of a school board meeting in Walterboro, South Carolina, at which some parents heatedly complained that their children were coming home with bruises on their bodies as a result of being slapped, rapped over the knuckles and hands, and paddled with unnecessary roughness. Mothers charged that their kids had been physically punished for having made mistakes in their homework. One of them reported that her child, who has an asthmatic condition, had been beaten on the hands and had suffered an attack the next day. Although she had previously explained the child's condition to the school principal, the teacher wielding the paddle had nonetheless hit the girl's hands so hard "that they nearly cracked."

A school official at the meeting assured the mother of the asthmatic child that "it won't happen again," but his superior hastened to remind the assembly that paddling "within reason" is legal in South Carolina. Accordingly, children in that county still have to depend on how any given teacher or principal defines reasonableness.

Toward the end of that school board meeting in South Carolina, an elementary school principal rose and said feelingly that he cared very much for children, and always had during his twenty years as a teacher and principal. However, he added, love for children must also encompass discipline and, the way the world is, among the kids he loves most are those who most need discipline. And that's why it is necessary, out of love for the children, to retain corporal punishment.

Around the time I heard of this South Carolina educator's palpable love for children, I saw the testimony of a representative of the American Civil Liberties Union before the Los Angeles Board of Education. Citing many complaints by parents about corporal punishment in the city's schools, she told of one father who charged that his son had been hit with a stick because he had put his foot on a desk while tying a shoe. Another time the boy had been whammed on the head with a book. Yet another loving way of implanting learning.

From a former teacher in Kansas City, Missouri: "I have witnessed the use of physical punishment with paddles and switches in the Kansas City metropolitan area schools. Principals have even punched, kicked, and smacked youngsters. I have seen an assistant principal use his belt on a boy, and a teacher throw a set of keys into a child's face. When a youngster tries to protect himself, he's sent to court and then, on occasion, to reform school. I finally had to stop teaching. I couldn't take watching that go on and on and on."

A teacher from Kettering, Ohio, reports that "in fifteen years at the eighth grade level, I had paddled three times, and I am deeply ashamed of those times. But during these years, I have seen so much violence against children by other teachers and by administrators. There was one boy whose head was knocked against the wall hard when an assistant principal happened to walk by and overhear the boy's teacher saying to someone that the boy's attitude had deteriorated and she couldn't explain why. That's all the assistant principal had to hear. He simply walked into the room, pulled the boy out, and knocked his head against the wall."

So much for children as "persons" under the Constitution, the Supreme Court notwithstanding.

In Mesquite, Texas, a mother, having enrolled her children in elementary school, tells the principal that while she is against corporal punishment for all kids, she is expressly concerned that one of her children never be hit under any circumstances because the girl has a pin in her arm from a horse accident. The mother has been warned by doctors that if the arm should be reinjured, the child could lose it. Soon after, during one day in school, three of the woman's children—including the one with a pin in her arm—are beaten.

The mother immediately contacts Citizens Against Physical Punishment (a Dallas group that has long been trying to abolish corporal punishment), and she is advised to take the children to the hospital for examination. There they are treated for severe bruises. One has a knot in his side where the principal struck him with a twenty-two-inch board. The next stop is the child-abuse section of the local child welfare facility. The

mother is told there that although pictures will be taken of the
children as proof of the harshness of the beatings they have
received, child welfare personnel are not empowered to "interfere" with the public schools. They can intervene directly only
in *parental* child beatings. The mother is told to take the pictures and call the Mesquite Police Department so that she can
file a complaint. When the police arrive at her home, they
begin, with guns drawn, to search the premises as one officer
keeps asking the mother, "Are you still going to file charges
against our schools?"

In New York City, where corporal punishment is forbidden
by the Board of Education, kids nonetheless keep getting hit.
One of many reports I have received from teachers and former
teachers in the New York City school system is this one from
a woman who taught in largely black and Hispanic schools:

> For two years I worked in a school where I witnessed physical
> force being used on male students by at least three or four
> male principals. By physical force I mean arm-twisting,
> headlocks, other wrestling holds, and chopping at the neck
> with the side of the hand. At another school, where I did per
> diem work, a teacher took out a ruler, which she said she
> often used, and struck a boy twice, hard. *He was a first-
> grader.* What I saw in both schools is fairly typical in so-
> called rough schools. In many cases, a white teacher will
> perpetrate this on a non-white student. In the case of the
> first-grader, it was a black teacher hitting a Hispanic stu-
> dent. In some schools, it is often black on black, which, in
> some way, appears to be more acceptable. *But what way is
> that?*

Of all the reports of corporal punishment I have seen and
verified, one of the most affecting concerns a high school senior
in Dallas in the early 1970s. The boy had a good academic
record, an A in conduct all the way through school, and the

kind of self-discipline that enabled him to hold down a job while going to school so that he could pay for his own car.

Arriving at school one morning, he parked his car in the wrong place. His punishment was to be three blows. When he refused to take physical (and concomitant psychic) abuse, he was suspended for three days. He was further told that he would not be readmitted to the school unless he took those three blows.

Here is a letter to an administrator of the school from the young man's mother:

I have no quarrel . . . regarding your right to punish my son for violating a rule of parking in the school parking lot. It was a careless act, and he is aware that I am very displeased that he should cause all of us trouble by violating such a simple rule. A three-day suspension seems to me to be adequate punishment for this first violation, but we would accept whatever additional suspension or other punishment you deem proper—short of corporal punishment—and we assure you that this violation will not occur again.

I am morally opposed to corporal punishment. I consider it archaic, barbaric, and counterproductive to all the values I believe parents and teachers should try to promote in their young. It could only serve to degrade and humiliate my son without teaching a lesson of any humane value. In my opinion it would equally degrade the person administering the blows. It is a lesson in might makes right, which I have taught against as long as my son can remember. It may be a small matter to you, but it is basic to my deepest beliefs and those I have taught him.

I know that you have called him into the office a number of times in regard to his hair and, as I have written you previously, I do not think his hair is attractive, but I do not think it disruptive to the school and I think it should be a matter of personal choice. However, I have told him previously that I would not do battle over his hair. Indeed nothing is more difficult for me than to do battle at all, and I will not do it for what I judge to be minor causes. Except for his hair, my son has given no one any trouble. He is a gentle person, intelligent, hard-working, and mature for his age. Do you sincerely believe that the best way to deal with young men is by humiliating them?

Perhaps you do not consider him a young man and I will not belabor the point that the Draft Board disagrees. If you consider him a child, then perhaps you would agree with the laws recently enacted in some states that parents are responsible for the acts of their children. I do not mean to be facetious when I say that, as the one totally responsible for my son's beliefs—that is, that he has a right to retain some dignity and refuse to be whipped like a slave or animal—I am the proper person to whom you should deliver your blows. I am willing and would receive them without taking the matter any further.

It is, of course, most important to my son, his father, and me that he be able to complete the few short months before graduation. We fully understand that you have it in your power to deny him this important event. I ask that you please consider alternative punishment if the three-day suspension is not sufficient. Surely you do not dislike him this much and if so, may I try to understand why? In any case, I could never give my consent to anything as distasteful and repulsive to me as having you humiliate him by striking him. I find it almost impossible to believe that anyone could seriously believe that such methods of punishment are constructive and helpful in any way.

I ask you to please reconsider.

The school authorities refused to reconsider.

The boy, after days of anguish, broke down for the first time and told his father, "Dad, I want to finish school." The father and his son went to the school and the father watched as the boy took the three blows. The boy went on to class and did get his high school diploma, with an extra learning dividend.

Two court cases provide additionally harsh illumination on the theory and practice of corporal punishment in the public schools. In *Ingraham* v. *Wright,* tried before a United States district court in Miami in the fall of 1972, James Ingraham testified that from elementary school on, he had often been paddled by teachers and administrators "to help me learn." In October 1970, while a student at Charles R. Drew Junior High School, Ingraham, forced onto a table by two assistant principals, who held his legs and arms, was hit more than twenty times with a paddle by the school's principal. When the boy came home, his mother took him to Jackson Memorial Hospital, where a doctor gave him pills to relieve his pain, advised his mother to apply cold compresses to the boy's blistered buttocks, and told him to stay in bed for a week. Ingraham did remain at home for a week, in bed, face down. His offense had been insufficient alacrity in getting off the stage of the school's auditorium.

During the trial, three witnesses testified that an assistant principal wore brass knuckles; and one of those witnesses, the mother of a student at the school, said she had seen that school official use his brass knuckles while administering discipline. Another witness, a fourteen-year-old boy, testified that a school administrator, in the course of punishing him for not taking a seat in the auditorium quickly enough—the student was trying to wipe grease off the chair—struck him with a paddle across his head. "I was begging for mercy," the boy said, "but he wouldn't listen. Then he took off his belt and hit me with the buckle." The witness then showed the federal district judge an inch-long scar alongside his left eye, the result, he said, of doctors at Jackson Memorial Hospital having had to open and drain a swelling on his head caused by the beating. When the youngster returned to school, his mother told school personnel that he suffered from asthma. Nonetheless, the boy was again beaten with a paddle, had an asthma attack, spat up blood, and was taken to a local health center.

In reporting on the trial, Ellis Berger, an education writer for the *Miami News,* noted:

Student witnesses say they have been paddled by teachers who did not first consult with the principal (such consultation is required by Dade County school policy). They testified to being paddled and seeing others paddled before the entire class and said entire classes were paddled when one unknown offender had stolen money or some personal item.

Girls as well as boys have been paddled by teachers and administrators with the rest of the class looking on. Two students testified to being paddled at Shenandoah Junior High by another student at the direction of an assistant principal.

They have testified about being paddled for being late, for skipping school, for chewing gum, for leaning back in their seat, for having their shirttails out, for talking, for standing up in class, for fighting, for being noisy in the shower, for not having the proper T-shirt or shorts or gym shoes in physical education class. The list of reasons for paddling covers about every possible "offense" by a student, according to sworn testimony.

The suit, brought by Legal Services of Greater Miami, included a count making it a class action filed on behalf of all students in the Dade County public schools. This count asserted that any form of corporal punishment in that county's school system is unconstitutional because it deprives the physically punished student of due process, equal protection of the law, and is, moreover, "cruel and unusual punishment" as prohibited by the Eighth Amendment.

On February 23, 1973, United States District Judge Joe Eaton held that while the plaintiffs had demonstrated "instances of punishment which could be characterized as severe, accepting the students' testimony as credible," and that "while the Court believes that corporal punishment may be administered in such a way that the resultant psychological harm to some students will be substantial and lasting," nevertheless "the use of corporal punishment by school authorities does not abridge any privileges or immunities guaranteed to students by the Constitution of the United States."

Accordingly, all counts in the plaintiff's complaint were dismissed.

The argument went on higher, and in 1974, the United States Court of Appeals for the Fifth Circuit held that in this case from Florida's Dade County school system—the sixth largest in the nation—there *had* been a violation of the beaten students' constitutional rights: specifically, their right under the Eighth Amendment to be protected against cruel and unusual punishment.

The decision did *not* outlaw all corporal punishment in the Dade County schools, but did specify that

whether punishment is cruel and unusual depends upon the circumstances surrounding the particular punishment. In this case children aged through 15 were punished for alleged misconduct that did not involve physical harm to any other individual or damage property. The system of punishment utilized resulted in a number of relatively serious injuries and thus clearly involved a significant risk of physical damage to the child. Taking into consideration the age of the children, the nature of the misconduct, the risk of damage, this court must conclude that the system of punishment at the junior high school was "excessive" in a constitutional sense.

The severity of the paddlings, and the system of paddling at Drew, generally, violated the Eighth Amendment's requirement that punishment not be greatly disproportionate to the offense charged. Our review of the evidence has further convinced us that the punishment administered at Drew was degrading to the children at that institution.

The court also held that there had been a lack of procedural safeguards—e.g., the students had not been given a chance to explain the circumstances that led to their punishment—and so the students' rights to due process of law had also been violated.

In a way, even though the court had not declared corporal punishment per se unconstitutional, this would have been somewhat of a breakthrough decision in view of the reluctance so far of nearly all other courts to find *any* constitutional violations in the use of corporal punishment on schoolchildren. However, the same case, *Ingraham* v. *Wright,* was submitted once again to the United States Court of Appeals for the Fifth Circuit, *en banc,* in February 1975; and alas, in a decision handed down in January 1976, the moderate breakthrough was rescinded, as the majority of the court decided that the Eighth Amendment cannot apply to corporal punishment pounded out on schoolchildren. Nor was the Fourteenth Amendment (due process) applicable either.

Judge Rives, in a forceful dissenting opinion, in which he was joined by two other judges, provided a level of constitutional reasoning in cases such as this, which ought to be studied by the Supreme Court.

I cannot escape the conclusion that these school children have a constitutional right to freedom from cruel and unusual punishment when applied under color of state law, and that it is our duty as federal judges to enforce that right. . . . The administration of cruel and severe corporal punishment can never be justified. The circumstances and severity of the beatings disclosed by the presently undisputed evidence amounted to arbitrary and capricious conduct unrelated to the achievement of any legitimate educational purpose.

As for the denial of the students' Fourteenth Amendment rights, Judge Rives emphasized that the undisputed evidence

shows deprivations of liberty, probability of severe psychological and physical injury, punishment of persons who were protesting their innocence, punishment for no offense whatever, punishment far more severe than warranted by the gravity of the offense, and *all without the slightest notice or opportunity for any kind of hearing.* . . . The brutal facts of this case should not be swept under the rug. Clearly . . . the plaintiffs have been subjected to cruel and unusual punishment. Under color of state law, they have been arbitrarily deprived of both property and liberty. Even more clearly, they have been denied procedural due process. [Emphasis added.]

The precedent to be set by the en banc majority is that school children have no federal constitutional rights which protect them from cruel and severe beatings administered under color of state law, without any kind of hearing, for the slightest offense or for no offense whatsoever. I strongly disagree and respectfully dissent.

(Conceivably, Judge Rives may yet prevail. The Supreme Court in May 1976 decided to consider whether the Eighth and Fourteenth Amendment rights of the youngsters involved in *Ingraham* v. *Wright* had indeed been violated.)

Even Judge Rives's rather advanced judicial reasoning, however, does not go so far as to abolish corporal punishment. This judge, like a few others, is indeed willing to consider taking some action against "excessive" physical force while maintaining the view that "reasonable" corporal punishment, under proper procedural safeguards, is permissible. The result of this kind of balancing is what Alan Reitman, associate executive director of the American Civil Liberties Union, calls a "floating" standard. That is, instead of abolishing corporal punishment entirely as a violation of a student's basic rights as a person under the Constitution, the question of the "proper" degree of force that can be inflicted on a child is left to the criteria of individual judges. Accordingly, as Reitman says, there is no "single defined standard that could be applied nationally." What is brutality to one judge can be well within an educator's disciplinary privileges to another.

The federal courts, including the Supreme Court, have continually muddied this issue in diverse other ways. In 1975, the Community Advocate Unit of the Pennsylvania Attorney General's Office asked: "If corporal punishment is to be prohibited as cruel and unusual punishment in prisons and juvenile institutions [as it has been in two U.S. Court of Appeals decisions], how is it constitutionally permissible in public schools? ... A common sense approach to the question must be: if you cannot beat prisoners or delinquent children, how can you beat children in public schools?"

Furthermore, as Pennsylvania's Community Advocate Unit points out, the Supreme Court's *Tinker* and *Gault* decisions have made clear that children are "people" under the Constitution. Therefore, "as people [under the Constitution] school children should be immune from an unconstitutional intrusion into that 'sacred' zone, the student's body." And by the same reasoning, schoolchildren should also be immune from cruel and unusual punishment and deprivation of due process.

To see how far the courts still are from these logical interconnections, there is the lamentably instructive case of *Ware* v. *Estes,* the Estes in question being the Dallas, Texas, superintendent of schools. In the plaintiff's original petition, the Statement of Facts noted:

A. On numerous occasions during the school year, 1969–70, Douglas Ware, a student at Sunset High School, was struck for allegedly disciplinary reasons [by a vice-principal and a teacher at the school]. And

B. On or about May 5, 1970, Roderick Oliver, a student at Sara Zumwalt Junior High School, was knocked unconscious at 4:30 p.m. [by a teacher at that school] for alleged disciplinary reasons.

Placing the court action in the context of constitutional law, the attorney for the students charged that the defendants—Dr. Estes, two principals, two vice-principals, and two teachers—had failed to give the students "any opportunity for a hearing, however informal, to present their side of the alleged misconduct before an impartial referee." Furthermore, the students had not been allowed to present witnesses or other evidence in their defense; could not question or cross-examine any witnesses against them; did not have the opportunity to be represented in any hearing (if there had been a hearing) by an attorney; and were not informed that they had the right to a notice of charges, a hearing, and representation.

In addition, the petition continued, "the infliction of corporal punishment by public school officials on public school students on its face abridges the 'privileges and immunities' of all such students . . . including their rights to physical integrity, dignity of personality, and freedom from arbitrary authority in violation of the Fourth, Ninth, and Fourteenth Amendments to the Constitution of the United States." The student plaintiffs also claimed that corporal punishment "deprives public school students of 'liberty without due process of law' in violation of the Fourteenth Amendment to the United States Constitution since it is arbitrary, capricious, and unrelated to achieving any legitimate educational purpose. On the contrary, the use of corporal punishment in the schools results in a hostile reaction to authority, breeds further violence and interferes with the educational process and academic inquiry." Moreover, corporal punishment "constitutes 'cruel and unusual punishment' . . . since it was grossly disproportionate to any misconduct Plaintiff-Students may have engaged in [and is therefore] in violation of the Eighth and Fourteenth Amendments to the United States Constitution."

On paper at least, the constitutional issues with regard to the legality of corporal punishment in public schools appeared to have been clearly joined in *Ware* v. *Estes*.

Before the case was tried, Marshall Ware, father of plaintiff Douglas Ware, wrote to Dr. Karl Menninger, whose book *The Crime of Punishment* had been published in 1968:

It is because two of our [three] sons have been subjected to physical punishment in Dallas Schools that we plead for your personal support to end the Crime of Punishment.

These sons are very different. Our third boy . . . has a minimal brain dysfunction symptomized by visual-motor problems, short attention span, clumsiness, and spelling/writing difficulties. Labeling this as "not paying attention" and "laziness" has resulted in spankings from the first grade—plus ridicule and the destruction of his dignity by teachers. Last September—fearing he would eventually be a dropout or emotional wreck—we placed him . . . in the Angie Nall School Hospital for Educational Retraining in Beaumont, Texas. . . . We hope to have this boy back home this fall but fear the problems which will arise with the public schools' policy of physical punishment.

Our second son Douglas (age 16, an excellent IQ, physically perfect and a champion swimmer, sensitive to personalities and hypocrisy) has the problem of being outspoken and can be profiled by the typical undesirable teenage characteristics as outlined by Gesell, Ilg, and Ames. The school, trying to train him with regular paddling, caused him to become a behavior problem, and his grades to drop (from B's to D's and F's) in all classes. He is now having regular psychiatric sessions. . . .

My wife and I feel that the causes for our boys being physically punished are just about as valid as spanking for pimples. We feel the root of this spanking problem can best be reached only by attacking the whole attitude and system of the schools in their dealing with and teaching students. . . . Our fight to eliminate corporal punishment is the most essential king-pin. It can force our schools to communicate, cooperate, and teach—rather than coerce. . . . If we are successful, it may be a milestone toward forcing an understanding of and solutions to the problems of revolt, dropouts, drugs, turned-off kids—even poor teaching. It can begin with the school setting a good example which will nurture an appreciation of our Constitutional rights and the dignity of man— and boys. . . . We hope you can give us some support.

Dr. Menninger responded by registering his appalled disapproval of what had happened to Mr. Ware's sons in the Dallas schools, but he was unable to testify at the trial. Professor David Gil of Brandeis University did appear for the students; and in an interview with the *Dallas Morning News,* Dr. Gil emphasized that "It's much worse for public schools to beat children than for parents to do so because the public schools set an example." He noted, for instance, that according to a nationwide study of child abuse he had directed in 1969 for the federal Health, Education and Welfare Department, the rate of child abuse per 100,000 in Texas was more than three times the national average (31.2 as compared with the national average of 9.3). In that state, where corporal punishment in the schools is especially widespread, physical abuse of children at home is also strikingly more prevalent.

During the court proceedings, the plaintiffs claimed—and they were not rebutted on the facts by the defense—that Douglas Ware had been hit more than twelve times (with a paddle, a tennis shoe, and a baton) for such misdeeds as not bringing his tennis shoes to class in the gym, not wearing a shirt in the weight room, talking back to a senior student, being late for workouts, not having his equipment in order, failure to pay towel fees, and failure to submit to a physical examination.

Intriguingly, one of the witnesses for the defense was a former principal of Sunset High School, who edified the court with the tale of Rufus Moore's tennis shoe. Mr. Moore, the former principal explained, had been a basketball coach at the school who whipped his players with the fabled shoe in order to motivate them to higher levels of performance and presumably to greater attainment of self-discipline. The shoe grew to mean so much to the boys, the witness added, that it was placed in a niche of honor in the school auditorium, where it remained until the building was remodeled. At that point in Dallas school history, Rufus Moore had become ill, and a number of Sunset High School students took the hardy tennis shoe to his bedside at Methodist Hospital in Dallas to provide a spiritual lift to the ailing coach.

The point appeared to be that Douglas Ware, rather than having been abused, had been involved in a noble tradition at Sunset High, and it was a mark of his further deficiency as a student not to have been aware of that educational blessing.

As for the other plaintiff in the case, Roderick Oliver, the court records show that a teacher at Sara Zumwalt Junior High School admitted he had indeed struck the sixteen-year-old boy and knocked him unconscious—but with his open hand, not with a paddle. Furthermore, he had done so not as a teacher, but as an individual in a fit of anger when the boy, according to the teacher, directed an obscenity at him. (The incident had resulted from the teacher's objection to the boy's desire to reenter the building after school for a drink of water.) In any case, following the attack, Oliver had been hospitalized for two days.

Upon deliberation, Federal District Judge William M. Taylor, Jr., found no substantial constitutional issues in the plaintiffs' charges. The United States Court of Appeals for the Fifth Circuit agreed with the lower court; and on November 20, 1972, the United States Supreme Court declined to hear an appeal of the rulings that permit personnel in the Dallas public schools to inflict corporal punishment on children.

Is there any likelihood that the Supreme Court might change its mind on this issue in the foreseeable future? It would hardly seem so, judging by the Supreme Court's affirmation in October 1975 of the constitutionality of Russell Carl Baker's having been hit with a wooden drawer divider by his social studies teacher. It is possible, however, that the high court, on the basis of its decisions requiring due process for student suspensions (*Goss* v. *Lopez* and *Wood* v. *Strickland*), will mandate some form of due process procedure for corporal punishment (as another form of school discipline). But these safeguards are almost certain to be minimal and will mean, for example, that the child will have to be given some kind of pro forma "hearing" before he is hit. But he will still be hit.

Therefore, while cases will continue to be brought through the federal courts (with the long-distance hope that a differently constituted Supreme Court may someday give schoolchildren the same right not to be beaten that convicts have), the emphasis in the years ahead by corporal punishment abolitionists will be on lobbying municipal and state legislators (who can still prohibit the hitting of schoolchildren). And a corollary drive will be toward the mass education of parents on the diverse injuries, psychological as well as physical, that are caused by corporal punishment in the schools.

Until fairly recently, there has been no central clearing house of information and support for those trying to end what Eric Sevareid joshingly calls kid-whacking in the schools. Now, largely through the determined efforts of Carolyn Schumacher (a resourceful, indomitable Pittsburgh mother of two school-children and a doctoral candidate and teaching fellow in American history at the University of Pittsburgh), a start has been made toward establishing a national organization to abolish corporal punishment in the schools.

In the late 1960s, while teaching in an elementary school on Pittsburgh's North Side, Mrs. Schumacher was asked by a colleague to be a witness while the colleague punished a boy in her class. "To my amazement," Carolyn Schumacher recalls, "the boy, just an ordinary, unassuming ten-year-old, braced himself against a desk while the teacher swung at him five times with a stick the length of a baseball bat, striking him across the buttocks, or thereabout, with all her might."

Upon further exploration, Mrs. Schumacher discovered that in many schools in Pittsburgh, "children were being slapped, pushed, and poked by teachers, and constantly threatened with a paddle that in some schools was either carried by the principal as he patrolled the halls or kept on public display in the office. Some teachers kept a paddle handy at their desks and carried it during bathroom recess as they trooped the children in silence to be 'watered.' "

In April 1967, Mrs. Schumacher helped form the Committee for Abolition of Corporal Punishment in the Schools. Its members recruited parents, social workers, and school volunteers to collect and verify incidents of corporal punishment in the Pittsburgh schools. In one sixth-grade classroom, for instance, as Mrs. Schumacher later reported, a boy had been caught making a paper airplane. Summoned in front of the class, he was told he had the choice of eating the airplane or being paddled.

He ate the airplane, and was then taken to the principal's office, where he was paddled anyway.

"I should add," Mrs. Schumacher notes, "that the boy in this case had a withered hand, did not have complete command of our language, and his father, a visiting scientist, had recently been in an automobile accident."

After amassing a considerable amount of evidence, the committee, despite resistance from the Pittsburgh Federation of Teachers, school supervisors, and various members of the board of education, finally persuaded the board to phase out corporal punishment in all grades of the public schools. But Pittsburgh's teachers, as I have noted, have never given up trying to get the board to change its mind.

"It is not only that corporal punishment abridges the rights of any kid who is hit," Carolyn Schumacher told me at an early stage of her battle in Pittsburgh, "but allowing it in a school also abridges the rights of all kids there, even those who are never hit. So long as it goes on in the school as a whole or in a particular classroom, kids who have not yet been hit live in constant fear of arbitrary and unexpected reprisal for real or imaginary offenses.

"Furthermore," she added, "many kids become accustomed to being used as the goat to frighten the rest of the children into submission and conformity." Sometimes, moreover, the child who is hit begins to see that as his role in class and makes a point of trying to get the teacher angry enough to paddle him. Whether for "attention" or other reasons, he continually makes a contract for misbehavior. Obviously, a child with that kind of syndrome needs help, not more hitting.

There can also be, Carolyn Schumacher believes, an addictive quality in the frequent use of corporal punishment. "In my experience," she says, "the teachers who use corporal punishment, or send children to the principal to be hit, tend to rely on corporal punishment more and more as time goes on."

I asked her reaction to teachers who say that parents have

told them they *want* their children hit if hitting is necessary to maintain discipline. After all, some of these parents say, that's what happens to the child at home, too, when he gets out of line.

"It's instructive," Carolyn Schumacher answered, "that hitting kids is one of the few practices that teachers do defend by invoking the wishes of parents. On the other hand, when parents inject their own beliefs concerning education, the normative teacher response, promoted in the training programs, is to invoke 'professionalism.' ('We don't do *that* because it is my *professional* opinion that it is better to do this.') But when it comes to corporal punishment, many teachers fall back on the claim: 'What else can I do? The parents *want* me to hit their children.'

"It seems to me," Carolyn Schumacher continued, "that the schools must serve a *teaching* function in this regard. They do not have to, and should not, reflect the worst aspects of the home. Especially with regard to physical violence against children. The student who lives with the notion that violence is sanctioned by society and watches other kids taken off to be beaten, or witnesses actual beatings, in the name of discipline, is getting the kind of training that you might expect in the schools of an authoritarian state. Think about it. What kind of citizen do we want to come out of our schools? If there is anywhere kids can learn to grow up to stand by passively and watch people being beaten, raped, and murdered in the street, it is in a school where children are brutalized by the people in authority."

The doughty Carolyn Schumacher, while working to end corporal punishment in the Pittsburgh schools, began to extend her proselytizing against the hitting of children. A member of the board of directors of the Western Pennsylvania chapter of the American Civil Liberties Union, she convinced that body to take a stand against kid-whacking; and she became one of the prime movers behind the decision of the national A.C.L.U. to hold a three-day National Conference on Corporal Punishment in the Schools in May 1972.

Commenting on that conference, *The New York Times* observed, in an editorial, "Spare the Rod":

One need not agree with the A.C.L.U.'s argument that the obnoxious practice violates the Constitutional provision that no person shall be deprived of life, liberty or property without due process of law. It would seem more consistent with common sense and humane considerations to prohibit corporal punishment simply because it is an atrocious violation of educational principle. It is ironic, as the A.C.L.U. points out, that corporal punishment may now be visited upon schoolchildren for the "crime" of talking without permission but not upon felons convicted of major crimes.

But even more appalling than such a legal affront to the status of children should be the thought that youngsters are being taught the efficacy of rule by bully. It is hardly surprising that such children subsequently apply that rule in their own dealings with others, weaker than themselves.

When, as a result of the May A.C.L.U. conference, the National Committee to Abolish Corporal Punishment in the Schools was formed in Dallas in October 1972, Carolyn Schumacher and Julian Hudson (a Charlottesville, Virginia, classroom teacher who had headed the National Education Association Task Force on Corporal Punishment) were elected to chair the committee.

Four years later, after continual failure to obtain foundation or any other support that would have enabled it to grow into more than a symbolic organization, the committee finally became part of a new national center for the study of corporal punishment in the College of Education at Temple University in Philadelphia. (Had the committee not been in existence, however marginally, there would be no center.)

Finally, for the first time in the history of American schooling, a research effort has begun to determine, with as much precision as possible, the full extent of corporal punishment in the schools with corollary analysis of the findings by educators, child psychologists, civil liberties attorneys, and other experts in related areas. There will also be extensive research on alternatives to corporal punishment, with particular emphasis on those being used in schools around the country—and on how to enable teachers to adapt to education without assault.

As will be shown in this book, there surely are alternatives, even with the most volcanic children in the "toughest" schools. First of all, there are teachers who, as George Dennison would put it, have so *earned* their authority in dealing with children that they don't have to use force to keep reasonable order. They know the kids believe them to be fair, and just as crucially, believe in their willingness to really listen to and cope with grievances.

Admittedly, there is not an abundance of such teachers. What of all the others? For them, alternatives to corporal punishment are myriad but require principals or teachers' unions that will arrange for a certain amount of breathing room for teachers.

For instance, Dr. Ruth Newman, an associate professor at The American University in Washington, D.C., and a resourceful researcher on group interrelationships in schools, has suggested that time be provided during the school week so that small groups of teachers who feel particularly beset in their classrooms can meet regularly to:

Lessen isolation and loneliness—two aspects of teaching which are usually uncared for by school officials and can eventually make for loss of control;

Look at one's own threshold of explosion—what particular kinds of behavior and language tend to make each particular teacher blow up;

Look at what is going on in each "difficult" child's life that makes him so impossible, unmanageable and provocative;

Explore ways in which the school staff can be deployed to take pressures off beleaguered teachers who feel likely to lose control.

Dr. Newman has other entirely logical, lucid suggestions; and since this is a book concerned with emphasizing common sense in schooling, here are a number of them, as presented by her at the A.C.L.U.'s National Conference on Corporal Punishment in the Schools:

Have crisis teachers trained in interviewing youngsters before [when the signs are evident], during and after blowups. Also have trained consultants to analyze specific teachers' blowups before, during and after their occurrence. That way, the teacher can learn to defuse himself before blowing up.

Develop, through school seminars, ways in which there can be greater desensitization to the usual provocative four-letter words.

Provide relief time, rest time and rooms, pleasantly set up, for teachers who, for the moment, have had it. Also have quiet rooms for children where *they* can cool off when pressures mount.

Have present, if a teacher is scared of his or her class, a backup person—an aid, volunteer, or extra teacher.

Schedule and reschedule curriculum to allow for active periods of play or gym after long periods of sitting or concentration, in both high schools and elementary schools, to allow outlets for everyone's body tension.

Discuss in class what means of control the children think work best for them, and why.

There are many other alternatives to kid-whacking, including, as the National Education Association advises, having "social workers, psychologists and psychiatrists working on a one-to-one basis with disruptive students or distraught teachers." To be sure, even if these support forces were available only part-time in the schools, their presence would add to the budget. But consider the question of cost priorities in this context. What is the cost of freeing a "disruptive" child now from his fears and frustrations so that he can learn; and what will be the cost, over the years, if he fails school and school fails him? (The question of how much, in dollars, we really do value schooling—and not only for the "disruptive"—will be explored in a later chapter.)

As for corporal punishment, the most effective way, of course, to motivate schools to find alternatives to hitting kids is to make corporal punishment flatly illegal. And that is the basic goal of the center for the study of corporal punishment at Temple University. Accordingly, one of its functions is to serve as a clearing house of legal briefs filed in corporal punishment cases throughout the country. It will also correlate and distribute information about ongoing attempts in cities and states to get laws passed prohibiting the beating of kids in school. In addition, the center provides both lawyers and lobbyists with access to a reference library and a roster of expert witnesses.

Unless there is a definitive Supreme Court ruling soon against corporal punishment in the schools—a most unlikely possibility, as I've indicated—it is going to take years of educating the citizenry at large before children are no longer the only Americans who can legally be beaten.

In North Carolina, near Gibsonville—where Russell Carl Baker was whacked with a wooden drawer divider by his social studies teacher for playing ball—Margaret Keesee of Greensboro tried some years ago, when she was a state representative, to convince the North Carolina Legislature to abolish corporal punishment. Not only did her bill fail to get out of committee, but when her seat in the legislature was next up, she also failed to win her party's renomination. Her revolutionary proposal had proved to be, as she put it, "political suicide."

Meanwhile the widely approved beating of schoolchildren continues, with some modifications. In October 1972, for instance, the school board of Aztec, New Mexico, abolished the use of rubber hoses for disciplining grade school pupils. Instead, it mandated a leather strap as the proper instrument of discipline in that town's schools.

And then there is the case of an elementary school teacher in Ottawa, Illinois, who was dismissed in 1973 because he used a battery-operated cattle prod on those of his sixth-grade students he thought required educational jolting. In May 1975, a state judge ordered the teacher reinstated on the basis, the jurist explained, that the administration of a cattle prod to a child's body is not "cruel" within the dictionary definition of the term.

Instructive in this matter is the fact that the board of education which had originally dismissed the teacher had not ever received a single protest against the use of the cattle prod from the parents whose children had been taught with this device.

Accordingly, for all the attention directed toward reforming the schools in recent years, it would appear that many parents and many school systems in the United States have yet to advance to the position taken by George J. Luckey, who in 1868, in his first report as Superintendent of the Common Schools of Pittsburgh, wrote:

We have found that teachers who govern themselves best could most easily govern a school. Those who prove to their scholars, by their moral deportment, their superiority, had the greatest respect shown to them. We have found that corporal punishment degrades a child in his own estimation. He loses his self-respect, and ... he loses his respect for his teacher.... Physical force is resorted to only by those who have aroused the bad passions of a scholar, and in turn, are under the control of bad passions themselves.... Not only is the old method of corporal punishment barbarous, but it also infuses an insubordinate spirit into the whole school, consumes a great amount of valuable time, unbalances the teacher's equilibrium and unfits him for teaching, turns the current of thought away from study to a hundred unpleasant reflections, and associates with school life most disagreeable scenes and incidents....

A man who tried hard to lift teachers, administrators, and parents to at least the level of understanding of children manifested by George Luckey in 1868 was the late Edward Ladd, a professor of education at Emory University. Together with Carolyn Schumacher, Carole Duncan (a long-time Dallas opponent of corporal punishment), and Alan Reitman of the American Civil Liberties Union, Ladd was central in the formation of the National Committee to Abolish Corporal Punishment in the Schools. In one of his last papers, Dr. Ladd urged his colleagues in schools of education to recognize that almost none of the current method books and other works on educational practices "so much as mention the practice of hitting kids." Ladd went on:

If we professors of education wait for bans to be imposed by school boards, most of us will have to wait a long, long time. Political bodies will not move significantly ahead of public opinion, and public opinion is not yet generally enlightened on this score. Courts in turn will rarely move ahead of the articulated opinion of members of the profession which, as has been pointed out, is still largely in the same unenlightened state. So it is we professors and students of education who should be taking the lead.

In the next few years, therefore, let us give "Discipline" and "Corporal Punishment" a larger place in our courses and in our conferences with students doing field work. Let us—some of us at least—give these matters a place in our research and writing. Let's get them on the programs too of the meetings of PTA's and lay groups. Finally, if and when court cases dealing with any aspect of discipline come up in our areas, let's offer to help lawyers prepare their briefs and offer to act as expert witnesses.

As yet there has been no significant response from professors of education.

The School That Reads

The principal is the head teacher, or so it used to be. He has long since escaped the classroom. A few may teach an occasional course, but most have only a roaming outsider's sense of life in the classroom for both student and teacher. Nonetheless, the principal is the key determinant of his school's ambience. If he considers corporal punishment, for instance, a destructive way of teaching, even the most dedicated kid-whacker on the faculty has to find other ways in which to discipline students.

Similarly, if the principal is flexible as to teaching methods, his school is likely to have a livelier faculty than most. On the other hand, it can be exceedingly difficult, as I have often seen, for teachers with even the most modest alternative proposals to make any durable headway against a resistantly traditionalist principal. It can be done, but it is exhausting work, and my perennial advice to new teachers, when there are jobs, is to make sure they know the principal's style in a given school before they apply to teach there.

All this is not to say that the particular style of a principal necessarily provides a sound way of predicting how much learning is going on in his school. I know of one chief executive officer of an elementary school who is so flexible he is positively rubbery. His school is a garden of learning options, a garden that has not been weeded for years. The children appear to be having a delightful time, and the teachers are relaxed, but when the school's graduates go on to junior high school, many of them turn out to be dismayingly deficient in reading and math. They are, however, most impressive in what they can create with construction paper. And I have been in the school of a principal who, in manner, appears to have willed himself into a caricature of Captain Bligh. In his tautly structured, no-frills school, most of the children learn at a quite satisfying rate. Except that he's not satisfied. He thinks it's too low.

What counts is not style but a principal's expectations of his teachers and of his student body. And that means, of course, his expectations of himself. The focus in this and the next chapter is on two principals of sharply contrasting temperaments and styles. What they share is an insistence that their schools work, and not just for the "bright" kids. Their professional performance *should* be the norm in this nation's schools. Instead, principals such as Martin Schor and Luther Seabrook are quite rare. And whose fault is that?

One afternoon as we were walking down the street, Paul Goodman turned to me and said, "Do you realize that if the ability to walk depended on kids being taught walking as a subject in school, a large number of citizens would be ambulatory only if they crawled."

Paul's comment came to mind during one of the recurrent debates among school people about why the schools are having so much trouble teaching kids to read—particularly the children of the poor. Is the fault that of this country's at least seven million functionally illiterate schoolchildren (according to George Washington University's Institute for Educational Leadership), or are the schools culpable? Reading may not be as initially "natural" a skill to acquire as walking, but is it as difficult to master as the schools make out?

This particular debate on the subject of who killed reading took place in the spring of 1973 when Wesley Miller, a professor of education at Queens College, touched off a fierce exchange of views in the Letters to the Editor section of *The New York Times* by stating flatly that schools are *not* to blame for low reading scores in the cities. The problem, he explained, is one of demographic changes. As middle-class families move to the suburbs, Professor Miller explained, city schools are left with an ever higher proportion of poor children. Furthermore, Professor Miller wrote, "I confidently predict that so long as New York City's present demographic trends continue, no remediation program will bring the city's reading scores up to national norms."

In one response to Professor Miller's letter, Dr. Kenneth Clark, then a professor of psychology at City College and a member of the New York State Board of Regents, charged Professor Miller with being "an agent in the perpetuation of the self-fulfilling prophecy that low-income and minority group children are not educable." Nonetheless, Professor Miller insisted in a second letter that "Like it or not, improvement in reading is going to depend much more on the elimination of poverty and the brutalizing environment than on remedial education."

A corollary and even gloomier thesis, which has been gathering adherents among analyzers of how children learn, is that between the start of a child's second year of life and the end of his third year, his learning patterns are irreversibly set. (Some say these patterns are set even earlier.) This bleak prophecy fails, however, to account for the often quite radical improvement in learning abilities among teen-age dropouts (or pushouts) who have been categorized as uneducable during their public school years but find that in a new learning ambience, created by principals and teachers with high expectations, they are not dumb after all. During the six years of independence of one such school, Harlem Prep in New York City (before it was taken over, at the brink of bankruptcy, by the city's Board of Education), 731 of its students went on to college.

Whether the public schools are to blame or the fault is in the children themselves, a dismaying number of Americans, not all of them poor by any means, are suffering from acute reading deficiency. (A 1975 U.S. Office of Education study indicated, for instance, that 22 percent of Americans over seventeen are illiterate and another 32 percent are only marginally literate.)

In their 1973 book, *Getting People to Read,* Carl B. Smith and Leo C. Fay (both associated with the Department of Reading at the Indiana University School of Education) point out that some 43 percent of elementary school children are in "critical need" of reading help, while at least 2.7 million high school students "cannot keep up with their classmates because of reading difficulties, and almost half of those in need of help in high school receive none.

"This dismal picture is even worse for minority groups in our culture," they write. "Persons of Spanish origin have an illiteracy rate of more than twice that of the whole population and eighty-five percent of black students read less well than the average white student."

Those teachers and school administrators (and there are many of them) who claim that a school can do only so much with youngsters beset by poverty and growing up in families that are "culturally disadvantaged," continue to be supported in their conviction, they say, by test results. The New York City public school system, for instance, has 1.1 million students. In two-thirds of the city's thirty-two school districts, blacks, Hispanics, and Orientals make up the majority of the pupils. However, the results of city-wide reading tests given in recent years indicate that only one-third of the city's 625 elementary schools have succeeded in having at least 50 percent of the children in their charge reading at or above the national norm. And in almost all those achieving schools, the student body is predominantly white. (By definition, half of all the children taking city-wide and national tests fall below the norm, and half rise above it.) In predominantly black and Hispanic schools, the majority of children not only do not read at grade level, but keep falling back each year. In one educational disaster area, Central Harlem, 87 percent of the elementary and junior high school students failed the standardized reading tests in 1975.

There are exceptions, however, among schools in severely "disadvantaged" neighborhoods. In one of them, P.S. 91, an elementary school in Brooklyn, where there are few white children and most of the students are from poor families, 51.4 percent of the pupils were scoring above the national norm when I first started to visit the school a few years ago, and the scores have since gone slightly higher. Although that is hardly a spectacular percentage, it is exceptional among "inner-city schools" (the encapsulating euphemism for schools that are largely non-white). Other elementary schools in the same district scored in the 20s and 30s.

Curious to find out how P.S. 91 is able to defy, as it were, those educators and social scientists who claim that only when the poor are no longer poor will their children be able to read competently, I went to Brooklyn to see what possibly wondrous techniques were being used in that school.

On the way, I asked the cabdriver what kind of neighborhood the school, at East New York and Albany avenues, is in.

"Let's say," he said, "it's mostly dark."

In addition to the rising black population in the area, Crown Heights, there are also Puerto Ricans, Haitians, Chinese, and a dwindling number of mostly middle-aged and elderly Orthodox Jews. Some streets are scarred by boarded-up stores and ravaged, abandoned automobiles; but there are busy bodegas, not so busy kosher butcher shops, and a store selling Hebrew books and religious objects, some of them imported from Israel.

P.S. 91, built in 1901, decidedly shows its age, but on an

overcast morning the first day I entered the rather forbidding four-story structure, the halls and classrooms were well lit and the atmosphere was markedly more cheerful than was the case in my own aged elementary school.

It was a few minutes past eight, and the principal of P.S. 91, Martin Schor, was talking with several teachers in a large outer office on the first floor. Meanwhile secretaries and other office personnel were briskly engaged in a variety of tasks.

Mr. Schor, a soft-voiced, balding, bespectacled man in his late fifties, with a round face and a habitually earnest expression, told me that we would first look around the school before he discussed, as he put it, his philosophy. The nature of the itinerary was clearly not a suggestion on his part. It was an instruction.

"The reason I can take time out during the day to show the school to visitors like you," Mr. Schor said, "is that I get in at six-fifteen. I have to in any case, so I can be sure, if one of my staff calls in sick, that I can get substitute teachers who are familiar with the school. My teachers have been trained to phone me at six-thirty if they're not coming in, and that gives me time to see that their classes are properly covered. I don't want my children to find a strange person in their room if I can help it. Also, by coming in early, if I have something to say to a teacher, we might talk over the counter here in the outer office. Otherwise I might have to interrupt his class later in the day. Then, too, I get a lot of paper work done before school starts."

I asked him how late he stayed at the school.

"Oh, I leave promptly at three," the principal said, "and I don't feel at all defensive about it. I have put in a full day. Nor do I usually do any schoolwork at home. If a principal is well organized, he doesn't have to."

Having left my coat in the principal's orderly inner office, I saw, as I came out, an assistant principal and a boy of about twelve, both seated in a corner of the large, bustling outside office. The boy's mother, a black woman with an impassive expression, stood and watched as the boy was being tested in reading.

"He's a new student, a transfer," Mr. Schor said. "As soon as a child comes here, we test his reading ability in the presence of his parent. We do that, of course, to find out what kind of group he should be in, but also so that the parent cannot blame us if she sees that her child isn't reading at the level he ought to be on. Then, too, it gives us a chance to ask her why she has allowed this state of affairs to go on so long."

"What kind of answers do you get?" I asked.

"They usually hem and haw," the principal answered. "But asking that question can help make them realize that they, too, have a role to play in their children's education. Then they are more ready to accept some of our suggestions about how the child can be helped at home. There are books and materials a parent can provide to stimulate the child to read, and we also ask the parents to check on whether each day's homework is done. They are very cooperative about that. The other day"—Mr. Schor smiled—"the parent of a child who was absent from kindergarten called to find out what his homework was."

As we walked out to the corridor, Mr. Schor said, by way of prologue to what I was about to see, "This is a traditional school. Any principal who intends to do an efficient job has to have an approach to teaching that suits himself and his staff. In the long run, of course, a principal will select teachers who fit in with his philosophy."

I asked him about the size and composition of the student body. "We have about 1,300 children," the principal began. "Well, the exact number, as of today, is 1,297. Some 81 percent are black; 6.6 are Puerto Rican; 3.7 percent have Spanish surnames but their parents come from other islands in the Caribbean; 3 percent are Oriental—mostly Korean, Japanese, and Filipino—and many of those don't speak English when they enter. That leaves 5.7 percent 'others.' The 'others' are white, and the percentage of them in the school keeps going down.

"As for the income level of the children's families," Mr. Schor continued, "many of the parents are on welfare or earn so little that their income is supplemented by welfare. The neighborhood is rough. Muggings and killings are not unknown. One parent showed up one day very distraught. Her husband had been shot to death the previous evening. He happened to have been robbing a store at the time. It was his own fault, but it was still quite a shock."

We talked about the exchange of letters in *The New York Times* some months before on the thesis that only a limited amount of learning skills could be developed in children from low-income families. "Regardless of what happens or has not happened at home," the principal said, "so long as we have the kids here in this school, we have to do our best. If a child has been taught to read at home, we're that much ahead. If he hasn't been, our responsibility is to teach him to read here.

"And we do," Mr. Schor said firmly. "There's nothing miraculous in the way we do it. When a school fails to teach reading, that's largely due to poor organization. We have, for instance, a special class for disruptive children, kids with emotional problems. Just one such child in a normal class makes it extremely difficult for the teacher to function. Most teachers aren't trained to deal with that kind of child. Currently there are thirteen students, third- and fourth-graders, in that particular class. *They* learn to read, too. And they are not necessarily fixed in that class. Last year, half the children who started in the room for disruptive children eventually moved into regular classes. As for the others, we keep trying hard with them, too. I run everything in my school, and everything I do is on a practical basis. I try to be honest with myself."

There was one other special class, I discovered. A room for non-English-speaking children from the third to the sixth grades. "It has been our experience," the principal explained, "that if we get a non-English-speaking child in kindergarten or in the first two grades, he can be assimilated with the other children. If he transfers here in the upper grades, however, he is likely to benefit from being in a non-English-speaking class. Otherwise he'd be lost in a room with thirty kids far ahead of him in reading English. But we do try to get them out of the non-English-speaking class as soon as we can. The kids are here to learn English. They have to face reality."

Proceeding along the corridor, the principal nodded from time to time at a teacher and sometimes at a child, but he clearly is not, as he is almost delighted to point out, a charismatic figure—an adjective he uses with evident distaste. By contrast, another principal I knew, Elliott Shapiro, while in charge of an elementary school in Harlem some years ago, was continually being stopped in the corridors and the schoolyard by children eager to show him their work or discuss a problem with him. Since there are few magnetic personalities in education, or in any other profession, Mr. Schor often emphasizes, it's necessary to work out a "viable teaching-learning situation" (a favorite phrase of his) in which averagely competent teachers and administrators can succeed with children.

As we were about to walk into a kindergarten class, Mr. Schor stopped. "You will see the children reading in there," he said. "Those we get in kindergarten, we start in on reading as soon as they are ready to learn sounds. We have three kindergarten classes in the morning and three in the afternoon. We stress phonics in this school. We do not teach the alphabet as such, because they don't need to know it in kindergarten. Teachers who spend months trying to get children to learn the alphabet by rote are torturing those kids. We save that time and concentrate instead on enabling the child to learn a few consonants at a time. When he has learned the sounds of eight to ten consonants, we start teaching long vowel sounds. After each long vowel sound is learned, the child in kindergarten goes on to learn how to blend the consonants he knows with the vowel sounds he knows. Learning to blend is the hardest part. It may take a couple of weeks. The important part of blending is the initial consonant and vowel. We're not too concerned about the final consonant, but if the child knows *see,* for example, and also knows *d,* he can and does learn another word. After a few consonant and vowel sounds are understood, the child is reading. We try to have that happen by January. At that point, the teacher will start making up little booklets and sheets of reading materials, using only familiar consonants and vowels. Long before Sesame Street, we were using stories similar to what are now being called Sesame Street–type stories.

"An important element in how we teach," Mr. Schor continued, "is that we use a concrete approach to teach sounds."

The principal interrupted himself to take a ring of keys out of his pocket. "We've had two robberies during which intruders invaded classrooms," he explained, "and so we decided to have a lock and key for all the classroom doors. At first, every teacher kept his door locked, but now some have decided not to. So far as I'm concerned, the decision is up to the teacher."

We walked into a large room brightened by boldly colored children's drawings all along the walls. One group of kindergartners and a teacher were gathered around a wooden tray which contained a lemon, a stick of licorice, lollipops, and a toy lion, among other objects that begin with *l.* The children looked up briefly to see who had come in, and then resumed the lesson.

"They're used to visitors," Mr. Schor said. "A lot of people have been around to observe, including all the other principals in this district. And the children are certainly used to me. I'm constantly going around, and that's another reason the kids and teachers are relaxed when I come in. It's not as if I appear once a year, and everybody's trembling at the visitation. Besides, the children are more interested in what they're doing than they are in us.

"You see"—he pointed to the tray—"decoding letters is an abstract thing. You have to use concrete materials to back it up.

According to Piaget, if children are continually getting concrete experiences with many different kinds of materials, what they learn is constantly being reinforced. Look over there."

Another circle of children and a student teacher were working at a wooden tray that had a cake of soap, a rubber snake, a soda can, a can of soup, and a small letter *s* on one side of a piece of construction paper, which, when turned over, revealed a large letter *S*. Both *s*'s had been made out of macaroni by a teacher.

"Some teachers use sandpaper to make the letters," Mr. Schor said. "Whatever the material, tactile learning reinforces other ways of learning. By the end of the period, these children, through these multiple experiences, can't help but know the letter *s*."

In a corner of the room I saw a boy with a large letter *B* hung around his neck holding hands with a little girl wearing the letter *E*. Mr. Schor saw where I was looking. "Each is pretending," Mr. Schor explained, "that he is afraid to say his name alone. But if they say their names together, they're a word."

Another group, with a paraprofessional in charge, was exploring a diversity of objects that start with *b*. As the paraprofessional, a slender black woman in her late twenties, pointed to a ball, she asked what other word beginning with *b* can be done with a ball. Four small hands shot up. The boy who was selected took the ball and bounced it on the floor.

"When it comes to a word you cannot teach by using concrete objects which the child can touch, taste, or smell," Mr. Schor said, "we act it out. For *run*, a child will run. For *knock*, a child knocks on the table. To teach the word *floor*, the teacher asks her children to put their feet on the floor. If they had learned the word *floor* by rote, they would not know as well later, when they see it on a page, what the word means. By the way, all these groups, except for the children working on math in that corner, are involved in word drills. But they don't know they're taking part in a drill. They're just enjoying it."

In the math corner, some of the children and a student teacher were using Cuisenaire rods (colored rods of different but related lengths), and others were making shapes out of geoboards. Sticking up from the geoboard are little pegs around which rubber bands can be put to form geometric shapes or to practice counting.

"The skill periods in the kindergarten classes," Mr. Schor said, "last about twenty minutes a day. After they work on reading and math, the children play with dollhouses, blocks, or clay. They also do finger painting, sing, listen to stories, and make things in arts and crafts. But the twenty-minute skill periods are very important. There are days when we don't have enough personnel so that all the children in the kindergarten classes can have their twenty minutes. When that happens, some of them play with blocks during that period. Some people call it creative playing. I don't. I want enough personnel so that every kindergarten child gets twenty minutes a day of reading and math. As it is, however, most of our kindergarten children *are* continually getting that sequential training in skills. When there is a skill to be learned, you cannot depend on a child being motivated by curiosity. If an adult is not there to make sure a child learns sequentially, the child may just sink where he is."

The children working on consonants with the black paraprofessional were now sitting around a tray of objects starting with *k*. Mr. Schor and I watched for a while. "She used to be a school aid who helped keep discipline in the lunchroom and patrolled the corridors," he said. "But when I see an aid with capacity, I try to work her into a classroom setting. Now she's going to Brooklyn College after school."

He walked over to the paraprofessional and asked her how many credits she has toward her degree. The answer was eighty-nine, and Mr. Schor looked quite proud of her and himself.

After listening in on a pronunciation session in which another group was engaged, I asked the principal on what basis the kindergarten classes were divided. "In the early part of the school year," he answered, "we may start a group with two or three kids who know the sounds of ten consonants. By December first, there could be seven or eight children in that initial group. A second group may be made up of children who know five consonant sounds, and so on. As the children learn more, they move ahead into other groups. Once they start catching on, they can move rapidly. There may be four or five units in one kindergarten class by the end of the year."

We left the kindergarten, and on the way to a first-grade class, Mr. Schor observed that because the neighborhood's population is decidedly mobile, fully one-third of each year's first-grade children have had no prior kindergarten experience. "Those who start with us in kindergarten and have succeeded particularly well," he said, "can, on their teacher's recommendation and my review, go into my top first-grade classes. Of those children who haven't started with us, most begin the first grade here lacking basic skills in reading. So they go into other groups. We have seven classes in the first grade. Right now the lowest class is on lesson eleven, and the highest is on lesson fifty-four. The kids in the highest group can pick up a book and read it independently."

"Do you use homogeneous grouping all the way through the school?" I asked. (Mr. Schor was somewhat defensive in his answer. The practice of grouping children according to their abilities—kids call them "smart classes" and "dumb classes"— is scorned these days by most educational reformers.)

"The trouble with heterogeneous grouping," the principal began, "is that the teacher loses the extremes in the class. The bright kids tune out because they're bored, and the slow readers lose more and more confidence in themselves because they can't keep up. When there is a narrow range of difference in a class, however, teaching becomes more efficient because the teacher can teach the class as a whole. In this school, each entire grade is considered as a huge classroom, and the children are grouped in homogeneous units within each grade. I know I'm going against the current literature, which charges that homogeneous grouping, or tracking, condemns slow children to a low track for life and is done out of discrimination. Here," Mr. Schor said dryly, "we're largely black, so we can't easily be accused of discriminating.

"Our way of grouping," he continued, "is not a lock step. The ability groupings are fluid and flexible. We are constantly making interclass transfers. As many as five hundred children in this school move within a grade into different groupings in the course of a school year. That way, no child is permanently tracked and, I might add, knowing that this is what we do presents a challenge to the child. As he succeeds, he is immediately rewarded by being transferred to the next better class. And wherever he is, he feels as good as any other child in the group. But putting a child in a heterogeneous class—where he feels he'll never be as good as the bright children—is like slapping him in the face.

"LOOK WHO GOT INTO THE FIRST GRADE!" said the brightly colored sign on the door of the classroom we had reached. Some of the twenty-six children looked up at us briefly; the rest continued to work. On a bulletin board at the back of the room there was a batch of original stories by the students. Skimming through the neatly written work, I was impressed by most of the young authors' sure sense of sentence structure and paragraphing.

I asked a boy in the back row if I could look at the book he was reading. It was a collection of stories, many from Aesop's fables; folk tales and nursery rhymes; and selections from Vachel Lindsay, Christina Rossetti, and Robert Louis Stevenson, among others.

"There are those who think reading is a mystery." The principal nodded toward the book. "But as you see, it isn't. I can pick out any child, and he'll read."

The principal beckoned to the boy whose book I had borrowed. Two tiny black girls sitting near him were also asked to join us in the corridor. Each of the three read fluently and with a quality of expression that indicated they thoroughly understood what they were reading. The fable was about a stork who, having been invited to dinner by a fox, nonetheless went home hungry. The fox had served broth in a large, flat dish. On the next day, the fox, having been invited to sup by the stork, in turn had to go home hungry. The stork had served broth in a tall, thin pitcher.

"You can never take comprehension for granted," Mr. Schor said, and proceeded to ask the children why the stork had gone hungry the first day and why the situation was reversed on the second day. The children told him.

"It's a lot harder to draw inferences," Mr. Schor observed as the children returned to their room, "than to rattle off facts. By the way, it's early in the school year, and the children in there are reading real literature, not Dick and Jane stuff. There's a peculiar theory, with which I don't agree, that inner-city children best relate to stories that mirror their own lives and neighborhoods. But the children here love these fables and tales and stories from another time. All kids do."

The book, I had noticed, is part of a reading program for the first six grades that is published by Open Court, a La Salle, Illinois, company that specializes in educational materials. "I chose Open Court," Mr. Schor said, "because it's an integrated language program, correlating spelling, grammar, vocabulary, and composition exercises. Each skill is constantly being reinforced by the others. As they learn to read, they're also learning how to write. Another advantage is that it's a sequential program. Most teachers, for some reason, don't know how to teach language arts sequentially. Furthermore, the teacher's manual for the Open Court program is simply written and thereby can be easily followed by any teacher.

"With the Open Court program," Mr. Schor continued, "most of the phonics the children need are introduced in the first year so that by the end of the year the child can read independently. We've adapted the program to our own needs—the acting out and dramatizing of words to strengthen comprehension is one thing we've added to it. And as a matter of fact, our stress on comprehension all the way through the program is greater than that demanded by the Open Court materials. What I also like about the program is that it has a lot of good literature. You saw what that first grade was reading. In the upper grades, the children read Aristotle, Shakespeare, Thoreau, Benjamin Franklin, Robert Frost, Langston Hughes, and Dylan Thomas, to name a few. There are also selections from Grimms' fairy tales, Jonathan Swift, and Lewis Carroll. As good as the Open Court series is, however, we also use supplementary reading materials from Science Research Associates; Scott, Foresman; Ginn and Company; and other publishers."

Coming toward us along the corridor was a group of about eighteen children led by a teacher. While the kids were hardly silent and the line was a good deal less than even, the firm but not unkind teacher was having no trouble keeping the peace.

Looking through the door of a second-grade classroom, I saw a teacher giving dictation. The door was not locked, and we went inside. On one child's paper I saw *endure, haughty, peasant, startled, foment.*

"You don't usually get words like these in the second grade," Mr. Schor said, looking over another child's shoulder.

On one side of the room, attached to a bulletin board, there were book reviews by the children and some original stories, which they had also illustrated. Turning, I saw a fourth-grade reader on the desk of a boy who was seated near the bulletin board.

"We give the children fourth-grade material in this class," the principal said, "for supplementary reading and for homework."

Down the corridor, on the door of another second-grade room, a large, hand-lettered sign announced: "A HANDSOME CLASS GREETS YOU!"

In the room, two children were listening with earphones to a programed math tape; two were writing a composition; three were working on a math lesson with a student teacher; two were deeply involved in a spelling game, making words out of a boxful of individual letters; three were reading a story while following its action on a film strip; and one boy was helping another with a math problem. The regular teacher was taking a large group through a reading lesson; and in the back of the room, a student teacher was working with one child.

The room hummed with activity, but the noise was never so loud as to interfere with any of the diverse undertakings going on.

"Do they look unhappy to you?" Mr. Schor asked. "Do they look downtrodden? Are they sitting with their hands folded? Are they dehumanized?"

I wondered at the line of questioning because the children clearly did not fit any of those descriptions.

"Well," the principal said, "sometimes I feel guilty running this kind of school. Even though we're succeeding, I feel I'm doing something wrong because so many of the current writers on education insist that all traditional schools are repressive and dehumanizing. This is a traditional school in that we have a lot of structure and we demand that everybody learns, but we do make learning come alive."

Leaving the second-grade class, we walked upstairs. In a corner of the corridor, outside a third-grade classroom, a student teacher was seated, with five children around her. "That's the way she likes to work with kids who need help in reading," Mr. Schor said. "It's O.K. with me so long as the kids do get help."

"On this floor," I said, "it looks like an open corridor school."

"We use the corridor," Mr. Schor instantly corrected me, "because we need the space."

Inside the third-grade room, I stopped to look at a wall of children's drawings among which were interspersed prints of paintings by Renoir, Léger, and John Marin. A sign, taped on top of the exhibition, asked: "DO YOU KNOW THESE MASTERS?"

"Look over here," the principal said. On a table near the window, there was an exhibit of various animals and masks that had been made by the children. "This"—Mr. Schor pointed to a dog ingeniously made of paper cups, scraps of mohair, and wire—"is José's pink poodle." José, watching, politely acknowledged our praise of his work. Walking past several African masks that had been made by the children and were now on the wall, I saw a number of pieces of unfinished pottery in one corner. "They're just beginning to learn this," Mr. Schor said. "We only got the kiln last week."

As two large groups of children continued their reading lessons, one with a teacher and the other with a student teacher, Mr. Schor led me again to the wall of drawings. "You don't see this kind of work in an elementary school," he said. "You don't even see it in a junior high school. I know. I've been an assistant principal in one. Look at the variety! This is a favorite of mine." He pointed to a finely drawn, delicately colored sketch of a circus acrobat balancing himself on a horse. "Four of our children," Mr. Schor said, "have won scholarships to Saturday art classes at the Pratt Institute. Very few schools in this city have even one child going to Pratt.

"You see"—Mr. Schor looked at me—"it's not only reading in this school. We also place stress on math, social studies, science, and on creative arts and crafts. There's a lot of enrichment going on throughout the whole school. More of our children, for example, are playing musical instruments than you'll find in any other elementary school in this city. Eight classes are getting instruction in strings, woodwinds, and brass, in addition to the seven first-grade and two second-grade classes that are involved in a new experimental program in learning to read music and understand rhythms. We also have sixteen classes getting French—from the first to the sixth grades—and that's the most for any elementary school in the city. We can do all of this—the reading and everything else—because we are properly organized."

A while later, in what Mr. Schor had characterized as a slow first-grade class, a teacher had just written *lazy* on the blackboard.

"Do you know anybody who is lazy?" she asked the class. Nearly all raised their hands.

"How do you know that person is lazy?" the teacher said.

"It's my brother," a little girl answered. "He stays in bed all morning."

"Yes, that's lazy." The teacher smiled. "Now, what does a bird do?"

The hands were up again. The teacher nodded to a tall, thin black girl. Staying in her seat, the girl extended her long arms and flapped them.

"Right," the teacher said. "They flap their wings. What kind of sound do they make?"

The room became a noisy aviary as the children's high voices filled the air in a spiral of "u-r-r-r-s."

"That sounds like a lion," the teacher said. "Go ahead again. I'm not afraid."

The birds having become children again, the teacher asked the meaning of *turn*.

A boy stood up, turned to his left, turned to his right, turned to face the back of the room, and turned to face the front of the room.

"If she were a more experienced teacher," Mr. Schor said softly, "she would have asked them for another meaning of the word—your *turn* in line. It's a more difficult concept than turning around or from side to side. But she's a good teacher. She'll pick it all up in time."

The children went on to make sentences out of *wings, flapping, turn,* and other words they had learned that morning.

One child, after successfully using the word *oil* in a sentence, observed that she had gotten the idea from a Sesame Street show she had seen recently.

"Sesame Street!" a chubby black boy said scornfully. "That's baby stuff."

"It is not," the teacher responded. "You learned *oil* in school just this morning, but she already knew it from Sesame Street. Is that baby stuff?"

The boy, not yet willing to yield the point, shrugged and grinned.

In another child's sentence, *strut* came up. "It ends in a *t*, right?" the teacher said. "Now, if a root word ends in a *t* and then I add the suffix *ed*, what do I have?"

"Strutted," several children shouted.

"Right. Show me what the word means," the teacher asked.

A small black girl in a blue sweater and a yellow dress rose and indicated considerable potential as a drum majorette.

Next on the agenda were songs in which suffixes and prefixes were added to a number of root words.

"We're not afraid to use words like *suffix* and *prefix*," the principal said as we were leaving the room, "if they belong with what the kids are learning."

On the next floor, we walked into a room in which twelve children were reading aloud from their books.

"This is the class for disruptive children," Mr. Schor said. I told him they didn't look disruptive to me.

"Oh, they have emotional problems, all right," he answered, "but they can read. We can teach anybody to read. It's a matter of efficiency."

"Isn't it also a matter of you and your teachers having high expectations of the children?" I asked.

The principal was silent for a moment. "Well, yes, of course. We feel that we can attack anything. This year I have seven first-grade classes, and the children in the slower ones will be reading fluently by the end of the year. I tell the teachers in

those rooms that I am in no rush"—the principal allowed himself a slight smile—"just so long as it happens by the end of the
year.

"The first year is crucial in reading," Mr. Schor continued,
"but when children come here later than the first grade, we
work with them, too, to succeed. However, if a child transferring from another school to our sixth grade is only reading on
a primer level, we can't do it all in one year. But we do what
we can."

Next door, there was a slow second-grade class, as Mr. Schor
described it. "Nearly all of them are new to the school," he
explained.

In front of the room, a little girl, who had to stand on a chair
to reach the top of the blackboard, was copying a paragraph
from a paper in her hand. The other children were checking
their papers against what the girl was writing, as corrected by
the teacher.

"They're learning proofreading," the principal said. "Having
everything interrelate is part of my philosophy. At one and the
same time they're learning listening skills, penmanship, word
identification, and proofreading. Each reinforces the other. In
this school, by the way, children start to learn proofreading in
kindergarten. From the beginning, they are trained to correct
themselves."

A few doors away, a small class of eight children was busily
engaged in a reading lesson. "Those are our C.R.M.D. children," Mr. Schor said, "Children with Retarded Mental Development. You'll notice that they have a full-sized classroom,
even though they are small in number. There is no reason why
these children shouldn't learn to the limits of their capacities.
I laid down the law about the C.R.M.D. class. I made it clear
that I wanted them to have a skills program, including reading.
In this school, we adjust to each child. And we instill a work
ethic in each child, because there is no other way to succeed."

Our next stop was to be P.S. 91's annex, an eleven-classroom, one-story structure across the schoolyard. It had been finished earlier in the year and has helped alleviate the overcrowding at P.S. 91. "This old main building, though, is not likely to be replaced," Mr. Schor said. "With the school population decreasing somewhat in this city, there will be fewer new buildings and much more repairing and extending of the old structures. I'd like to have a new building, but we can live with this one, especially now that we have the annex."

To get to the annex, we started downstairs. At a landing, we saw two small boys, carrying a heavy box, who had stopped to rest a few stairs below us. Mr. Schor moved to lift the box to the landing, and I joined him.

As we put the box down, one of the boys, looking up at us, said, "Thanks, but we were going *downstairs* with it."

"You see how you can make mistakes," Mr. Schor, deadpan, said, "by jumping to conclusions."

The gym was on our way, and walking through it, the principal motioned to a custodial worker. "A parent," he said "is complaining that the light bulb in the first-grade bathroom is out." The custodian began to explain why he hadn't been able to get around to fixing it yet. Without raising his voice, Mr. Schor interrupted him. "Get it done now," he said. The custodial worker nodded his head and hurried away.

Entering the annex, we met a group of children and a teacher who were going to the main building. "It's raining out," the principal told the teacher. "Some of those kids don't have coats." The procession turned around to get some coats.

We passed by an office painted in pastel shades and with new comfortable chairs and a new desk. "I wish I had that office," Mr. Schor said rather wistfully, "but one of the assistant principals is in direct charge of the annex. I have to keep my own office in the old building because I supervise the first and second grades—they're the most important—and the old building is where they are."

In a sixth-grade French class in the annex, the teacher, as is the case with many of P.S. 91's faculty, had first worked at the school as a student teacher. She was conducting the class almost entirely in French. Her twenty-nine students were black and Puerto Rican.

"Some of these kids," Mr. Schor said, "are as good as senior high school students studying French, and this is only an elementary school."

At the blackboard, a student had just written, "Je suis à mon ami maison."

The teacher looked quizzically at the sentence, and then at the class. A girl raised her hand. "Il a tort," she said.

"Alors?" the teacher looked at her.

"Je suis chez mon ami," the girl corrected the line on the blackboard.

"Très bien," the teacher said.

"This class," Mr. Schor told me, "can read eighth- to twelfth-grade materials—in English and French."

A few doors away, a teacher and a student teacher were working with one of the higher fifth-grade classes. The thirty-two children were arranged at six tables, and each group was focusing on a different task. There was a table for reading comprehension, another for creative writing, a third for pupils working with a Science Research Associates programed learning kit, and a fourth for students doing individualized reading. ("Each reads at his own level," Mr. Schor said of the fourth table, "and as the teacher circulates from table to table, she consults with each of them on particular reading skills they need help with.") At a fifth table, the children were involved in social studies; and at the last table, there sat the class's committee in charge of the week's social studies research.

"The way that sixth table works," Mr. Schor explained, "is that once every member of the class has decided which group they're going to work with, the class as a whole lists a number of problems to be solved. Each problem has a research committee assigned to it, and this week it's in the social science area.

The kids on the research committee go to the library, read books on the subject, question people, pool their information, and then share it with the class. They do not do all of their research on the outside, however. We require that some of it be done in school so that the teacher can see if they are acquiring proper research skills. Simply copying word-for-word from an encyclopedia won't do."

While we were in the room, two more students came in and found places at the tables.

"They've been at a meeting of the camera club," Mr. Schor said. "We have two camera clubs in the school; plus gym, science, and sewing clubs; and we have just started organizing a glee club now that one of the teachers has volunteered to supervise it. You see, the children are not held down. We find time for them to pursue their particular interests; but always, when a skill is involved, they learn under adult supervision."

On the way back to the principal's office, Mr. Schor was stopped by the assistant principal whom I had seen earlier that day as he was testing the reading ability of a student new to the school.

"He's a sixth-grader," the supervisor told Mr. Schor, "but he reads at a primer level. He's been back in Puerto Rico for the past two years."

"We'll put him in the non-English-speaking class," the principal said. "Even if he were to be placed in one of our slower fifth-grade classes, he'd be too far behind the other children. That's the kind of problem you have"—Mr. Schor turned toward me—"when you have a school that reads."

While the principal and his assistant were talking, I looked into a small, cozy room where a teacher and eight children were working on reading.

"She picked up those kids from a first-grade class," Mr. Schor said. "They're reading well, but they're getting some polishing in there. After this week, we'll need that reading teacher for the slower classes."

Back in his office, the principal motioned me to a seat. "Now," he said, "you're ready to hear my philosophy. It would have meant nothing to you if you hadn't seen the children first, and if you hadn't been to a lot of other elementary schools. You have, haven't you?" I assured him I had—urban, rural, open, custodial, and uncategorizable.

"First of all," Mr. Schor said, "a school has to be geared so that the average hard-working teacher can succeed. Teachers need success as much as the children do. If they are unable to get the kids to learn, they will begin to believe that it can't be done. And once a teacher has that idea, it *won't* be done. I don't doubt that a particularly brilliant teacher, with a lot of charisma, can make an open classroom—where, theoretically, each child follows his own interests—work for most of the kids in it. But just as in medicine and in law and in any profession, the elite are few. There are very few superior teachers. The teachers here are, for the most part, good; but I can think of only one who has the exceptional skills necessary to run a successful open classroom. Therefore, if an open classroom situation were to be imposed on them, the teachers at this school, like most teachers anywhere, would be doomed to failure from the start.

"All right, so how can the average hard-working teacher be enabled to succeed?" Mr. Schor asked the air. "By giving the teachers and the children all the help we can. Every class, for instance, has at least one other adult in addition to the regular teacher or it is broken up at various times during the day into small groups for which student teachers, paraprofessionals, and specialists provide additional reinforcement in reading and math.

"Furthermore," the principal continued, "all the children in our first-grade classes and in all the slower classes in the other grades receive daily reading reinforcement in small groups of eight for forty-five minutes. Special reading teams made up of teachers, or of teachers and paraprofessionals, or of trained paraprofessionals alone conduct those sessions in another room or out in the hall. When you're dealing with a teacher-pupil ratio of one to eight, a teacher can spot what each child needs in the way of help much more readily and can immediately work with the child, on a one-to-one basis, without worrying about losing the rest of a large class. And in an intensive forty-five-minute period, every one of the eight children can be reached many times. As I said, all classes in the first grade receive this special help, the bright as well as the slow. The bright ones, however, receive the help *first* so that more time can be provided for the slower students to mature. It makes no sense, and it can be quite damaging, to inflict pressure on slower children when they are not ready. A six-month period can make a lot of difference in the readiness of a child that age; and when he is ready, help will be much more meaningful and will be accepted without a sense of pressure.

"Our best teachers, by the way, are assigned to the first and second grades because in this school, we expect our children to be reading in those grades. Many principals don't start corrective reading programs until the fourth, fifth, or even sixth grade. In this school, I want as few kids as possible needing remedial help by then. Another thing we do is to organize our classes so that the bright classes are large, about thirty-two children, and the slow classes are small. Obviously, the slower children need more attention than the brighter ones do, and if a class is bright in reading and in other skills, a teacher can manage it even if it is large. On the other hand, I have a slow first grade now with twenty-one children. A lot of teachers would consider that a small class, but I intend to split it in half.

"All of this," the principal added, "needs a great deal of watching. I program my whole school with regard both to the use of teachers and other personnel and also to the placement of the children. My three assistant principals and I are continually checking on the progress the children are making. If one seems ready to move into a faster group, he's tested by me or an assistant principal or a reading teacher." Mr. Schor showed me a large clipboard to which organization sheets were attached. "Every week," he said, "this shows where the kids are and what they're reading. The information here is used to determine intra-grade transfers and also to indicate which books should be distributed where."

I was surprised and puzzled, I told the principal, to see the extent of the extra personnel he provides his regular teachers. In view of budget cuts made by the Board of Education in recent years, how did he do it?

"It's a matter of efficiency, of using your personnel well," Mr. Schor said. "For one thing, if a paraprofessional or school aid appears to have the capacity, I train her for work in the classroom rather than sitting in the hall on guard duty. By the way, since the school is going well, I've been cut down on the number of paraprofessionals I can have. That's a penalty for achievement. We also have a large number of student teachers from Brooklyn College, as many as eighty during some parts of the school year. They come here with their professors, and I've given them a room where they have their classes instead of having to go back to Brooklyn College. While the student teachers are at work here, I train them and watch to see whether they can produce. As a result, when there are openings in the school, I can cull the best from a large number of student teachers of whom I have direct knowledge. Most of the teachers here are young and most are former student teachers. That makes for added efficiency because those who come to work here full-time already know our routines and can concentrate instead on curriculum. Also, having already had experience in the school, they can work with a number of different groups in the same room without being fazed by it.

"Every new teacher," the principal continued, "is given an extra preparation period every day, whether she has worked here as a student teacher or not. The union contract already mandates that all teachers get one prep period a day, and for that period we ask a new teacher to volunteer to watch experienced teachers of particular skills on the same grade level as she's teaching—good teachers, for instance, of math or social sciences. For the extra period that *we* give her, I have her class covered so that she can watch a reading teacher."

I can understand, I told the principal, new teachers wanting to work extra hard, but I wondered how he motivated veteran teachers to keep trying to do their best.

"Aside from my giving them the kind of classroom conditions and materials that they can work with efficiently," Mr. Schor answered, "specialists often come around to give demonstrations, and the other supervisors and I are continually looking in and offering suggestions. There really is no mystery or mystique here. It's all hard work and organization. Oh, I also should mention that another source of help for our teachers is the sixth-grade students we use for tutoring. Every afternoon, for forty-five minutes, our top sixth-grade class breaks into small groups that work with slower children in all the grades."

I asked the principal how well the children from P.S. 91 do after they leave. "We feed into two junior high schools," Mr. Schor said, "and the reports from both indicate our kids do pretty well. That is, the ones who have been with us for some years. You see, our children want to learn. Attendance records are a good index of pupil morale. Last year, we averaged over 91 percent attendance; and in this school year so far, it's been higher.

"Another index of how the school is regarded in the neighborhood is that each year fewer parents send their children to parochial school. They're aware that we're improving. So aware, in fact, that there have been attempts to falsify children's addresses so they can get into P.S. 91. We now ask for a canceled electric or telephone bill to verify the child's address. The word is out that we're doing a job here. In this year's reading scores, by the way, 53.7 percent of our children were reading at or above grade level—a rise from last year's scores.

The percentage would have been higher except that in September, the Board of Education shifted almost a hundred kids from another school to this one. Just about all of them were reading below where they should have been, and we couldn't perform miracles with them between September and the following April, when the new tests were given."

"Is there much parent involvement in the school?" I asked.

"We try," the principal said. "We have a parent-teacher community council; we notify parents early and periodically if a child is not succeeding; there have been parent workshops; and the parents, as I've mentioned, know that we expect them to demand of their children that the homework be done every day. But as for sustained parent involvement, it's difficult. A great many of the parents work long hours, and others are so destitute they can hardly keep going themselves, let alone get involved in school affairs."

I was curious about Mr. Schor's own involvement in this school that reads despite the insistence of a substantial number of educators that since home environment largely predetermines how a child will do in school, many kids like those in P.S. 91 can't be expected to learn so well. Had he always been interested in working with children of the poor?

"No," the principal said. He had been born and raised in Brooklyn, he told me, and after going through the public schools in that borough, he entered City College in 1932, intending to be an accountant. "After my first year at City," Mr. Schor recalls, "it was clear to me that as the Depression deepened, there were no jobs out there for accountants. So I asked what field had the most openings. Teaching, they said. Then I asked in which subject teachers were most in demand. The answer was chemistry. So I studied chemistry." He was graduated in 1936 with a bachelor of science in education and chemistry. The next year, he received a master's degree in the teaching of natural sciences from Teachers College at Columbia.

Martin Schor's first job in the New York City school system was as a teacher-in-training at Brooklyn Technical High School. "Four and a half dollars a day," Mr. Schor said, "when you worked." After nine months as a civilian teacher of airplane ignition systems in the Army and a few months as a radar technician and discharge interviewer in the Navy, he returned to Brooklyn to teach in a junior high school. He then spent some eight years teaching science at George Washington Vocational High School, also in Brooklyn.

"I had to teach physics, chemistry, biology, nearly everything in the sciences that related to specific vocations," Mr. Schor explained. "And that's where my system of teaching reading began. Vocational high schools used to be dumping grounds. Where I taught, there weren't any textbooks because the kids couldn't read them. I had to make up my own curricula— chemistry for dental mechanics, chemistry for woodworkers, chemistry for plumbers, and so on. That also meant I had to get the kids to read well enough so they could do the experiments I had worked out. It was there I started working on experimental methods of teaching reading."

Mr. Schor went on to become an assistant principal of a junior high school in Brooklyn, where he stayed for nine years. "By that point," he recalled, "I wanted to work in an elementary school because I didn't know much about them. I went in as an assistant principal of an elementary school in Brooklyn; but since the principal took sick soon after I had arrived, I was acting principal of the school for most of my six months there. In any case, I learned as much as I could during that period. Voluntarily, I got myself involved in just about everything that was going on in that school. I even supervised girls' typing and health education classes. I worked in the library, and I supervised orchestral music."

"Are you a musician?" I asked.

"No," Mr. Schor answered, "but you can learn what to look for in a lesson so that it goes well. The point of my learning all areas of running an elementary school is that whatever a supervisor does has ripple effects throughout his school. If you don't know what you're doing, you can destroy a school."

In 1964, Martin Schor took over as principal of P.S. 91. His wife, Esther, who has been in the New York City public school system as long as her husband, was a kindergarten teacher when they met. She kept rising through the system, and since 1966, Mrs. Schor has been an early childhood supervisor in the Bedford-Stuyvesant schools. Her responsibilities include the training of teachers, principals, and assistant principals who work with children from kindergarten to the sixth grade. Her own specialty is the teaching of children from kindergarten to the second grade.

Married since 1940, the Schors have a daughter, Deta, who is a graduate of Brooklyn College with a degree in education. She has been a student teacher in two Brooklyn schools; and on her own time, has worked with experienced teachers in her father's school.

In view of his own considerable experience, and his achievement at P.S. 91, I asked Mr. Schor if he had any interest in training teachers at a college or university.

"Oh, I've had some offers," he said, "but I only have a few years until retirement."

So long as he is on the job, however, the principal of P.S. 91 continues to expect high levels of achievement from the staff and the children. He also expects the staff to be honest with themselves as well as with the children and their parents. In a recent issue of a monthly bulletin that the principal prepares for his faculty, there was a note concerning report cards: "They should reflect actual grade level achievements in math, reading, and spelling, and should contain specific suggestions for help, as needed. . . . *Do not* mark a child 'good' or 'excellent' if he is doing below grade level in math or reading."

The bulletin also informed the faculty that "report cards in Spanish are available for pupils with non-English-speaking parents." As for a forthcoming series of meetings between teachers and parents, Mr. Schor told the faculty to indicate to parents specific learning areas in which their child is in need of help. "And give specific ideas as to how the parents might help the child."

Mr. Schor, I also noticed in the bulletin, is working on parent as well as teacher accountability for how well or poorly the children do in their studies. "Parents were given word lists," the bulletin reminded the staff, "and were asked to help their children to learn this sight vocabulary. Please test your class on December 3, and on April 1, as was indicated in the letter to the parents."

The lead items in the bulletin had to do with suggested faculty reading in such professional journals as *The Instructor* and *Arithmetic Teacher*. In the current issue of the latter publication, Mr. Schor had listed, among other articles, "page 537— 'Activities in Math for Prekindergarten Children'—good for our kindergarten children." The staff's attention was also directed to page 591 of the same magazine—" 'Teaching for Generalization' an array approach to equivalent fractions— excellent."

The bulletin included a command from the principal: "Reminder—New York State Bulletins on Language Arts K-2 are excellent. They are *must* reading to provide you with an overview of skills that you might not be aware of, and a variety of activities and games that might be used to develop these skills."

The journals from which Mr. Schor draws his reading suggestions for the monthly bulletin are available in the school's library, along with a large number of other education magazines to which the school subscribes. Mr. Schor goes through all of these periodicals to find material for the bulletin. "I consider these suggested readings," Mr. Schor told me, "to be part of the continuous teacher training that ought to be going on in all schools."

Soon after one of my visits to Mr. Schor's school, I attended several of the events that the New York City Board of Education had scheduled for what it called "A Focus on Reading Week." At one of them, held in the board's Professional Library at its headquarters in Brooklyn, Mr. Schor was on a panel with several professors of education, a man from the New York State Education Department's Bureau of Reading Education, and Dr. Edythe Gaines, at the time the board's executive director of educational planning and support. Chairing the panel was Dr. Seymour Lachman, then president of the Board of Education. In the audience were principals, teachers, a representative from the teachers' union, and a number of professors of education at various colleges and universities in the city.

Dr. Lachman began by urging all those present to join him in "building a floor on which a child can reach the ceiling and perhaps move out by letting fresh air in the windows." I tried to picture the metaphor and could only relate it to Alice in Wonderland after she had eaten that side of the mushroom which made her so tall she was out of sight.

My attention wandered during the first two presentations, but I was brought back to the matter at hand by a startling announcement from the New York State Educational Department's reading expert. "We have research which proves," he told us, "that you get back from the child what you put into the child."

A friend of mine, a former New York City community school superintendent who is now a professor of education, leaned across the aisle to ask me if I thought that research project could possibly have been brought in for under a million dollars. I told him it must have cost a lot more. A few minutes later, the state Bureau of Reading Education's representative delivered himself of another revelation. "The evidence is beginning to show," he said, "that perhaps the crucial education decision-making point is in the classroom, in the relationship between the teacher and the students."

"That never occurred to me," my friend said solemnly.

Another panelist vehemently urged that "children be taught to attack print aggressively." There might be dangers in that approach, I thought, as Alice, being attacked at her trial by the pack of cards, again came to mind.

Dr. Edythe Gaines was next. A forceful black woman, who had risen steadily in the school system during the past three decades, she observed somewhat sardonically that "this Focus on Reading Week is like Mother's Day. But we must love mother all year long, not just for one week."

Avoiding rhetoric, jargon, and euphemism, Dr. Gaines emphasized her conviction that "fluency in reading should be expected by the end of the first grade. We ought not to be remediating forever. There should be no lower standards for the new minorities in the city than existed for earlier minorities. Furthermore, since most of our children in the new minorities fall within the normal intelligence range, there is no reason why they should not be able to read no matter what their neighborhood and their family life are like. It would be great, for instance, to have all the kids in our schools well-fed, well-clothed, and with a great deal of learning support at home. But for those children who don't have these advantages, the least we can do is to make them literate. Children who have already been victimized by poverty should not also be victimized by the schools."

When it was Mr. Schor's turn, Dr. Lachman said that it was his pleasure "to introduce to you the miracle worker, the principal of P.S. 91, where most of the kids are reading above the national level."

Mr. Schor, who had winced at the term "miracle worker," rose and corrected the president of the Board of Education. "Actually," the principal said, "53.7 percent of our children are on grade level or above. So that's not *most* of the children."

After having given a short summary of his educational philosophy and of how it is applied at P.S. 91, Mr. Schor concluded by saying, "There is no big triumph going on at P.S. 91. We're not doing as well as we should. We need more help in terms of personnel. But we are reaching the children, and the children are learning what it is to succeed."

Among the questions and statements from the audience, after the panelists had spoken, was a charge by Wesley Miller (the poor-kids-will-always-be-poor-readers professor of education at Queens College) that in reaction to growing pressures on New York City schools to raise the reading levels of their students, a lot of coaching for the city-wide reading tests is going on as well as increasing falsification of scores. And in some schools, he added, the poorest readers are excluded from the tests.

At one point in the discussion that followed the accusation, Mr. Schor calmly invited all those present to visit his school if they had any suspicion that his children's test scores had been in any way rigged. "We're not afraid of the most skeptical visitors," he said. "I invite any of you to give a reading test to our children. I invite any of you to ask any of our children to read and to answer questions about what he has read. We have nothing to hide."

Leaving the library as the meeting broke up, I heard a woman, who trains aspiring teachers at Brooklyn College, complain to a colleague, "I don't doubt that the scores at Marty Schor's school are accurate. But what bothers me about that place is that it's all business. P.S. 91 could be a lot more humanized than it is."

The colleague, also a woman, obviously had no patience with the complaint. "The greatest act of humanity that a principal and his teachers can perform," she said, "is to enable the children they teach to feel competent when they go out in the world. And that's exactly what Marty Schor is doing."

Turning a School Around

During the fervent doctrinal disputes among educational reformers in the 1960s, nearly all shared one article of faith—
learning should be child-centered, not teacher-centered. When
I attended elementary and secondary school, on the other hand,
we all pretty much learned what the teacher wanted us to learn
when she wanted us to learn it. The notion that each of us had
different styles and rhythms of learning would have struck the
faculty of the Boston public schools as comically irrelevant,
even if true. There was neither time nor additional personnel
to stop the assembly line; nor was there any principal with the
imaginative skill of a Martin Schor who knew how to trans-
mute the assembly lines.

Accordingly, kids were indeed damaged by procrustean
teachers. Some of my classmates now selling shoes or working
at middle-level civil service jobs had the intellectual capacity
to stretch themselves much farther; but fairly early on in
school, as they kept falling behind the pack, they convinced
themselves they were inferior material so far as learning was
concerned. They were "tracked" for life, even though they were
white and Jewish.

During the whirlingly high expectations of school reform in

the 1960s, child-centered learning, therefore, made obvious sense to me. Start with the child where he is, where his interests are, where his particular way of learning points. But then considerable numbers of radical school critics decided that if the child was in public school, the obstacles to his being truly recognized as an individual were so endemically huge that he had to be removed from the public school. And so there grew the "free school" movement, in which children would be transformed from passive prisoners of deadening schooling into independent, inquiring, self-motivated learners—all of this happening outside the dread official system of schooling.

Alas, there was hardly any place in the "free school" movement for the kinds of kids who made up the student body of Martin Schor's elementary school in Brooklyn. The new schools were "freeing" white middle-class children (with occasional token admixtures of "minority" kids). Many of the parents and teachers in the "free schools" would have preferred this to be otherwise; but they assuaged their guilt by believing —passionately believing—that the revolution of which they were so spirited a vanguard would ineluctably spread across the land, in time freeing all the black, Puerto Rican, Chicano, and white kids who had been left behind in those stockades called schools.

But the equal-learning-opportunity apocalypse never came. The public school buildings, many of them at least a half century old, still stand. Most of the "free schools" have disappeared. Without public funding, these schools had to scramble for evanescent foundation funds and other private backing. As a result, their average life-span has been some eighteen months. As the ancient Afghanistani adage says, those who would bring a revolution must themselves have the wherewithal to survive.

In desperation, some of the floundering "free schools" have tried to obtain public funding, but only a few have even marginally succeeded. As a 1974 Ford Foundation report on alternative schools, "Matters of Choice," has pointed out, "Although no Constitutional barrier exists to spending funds on private *nonsectarian* schools, legislative and political inhibitions usually prevent such expenditures. Because the overwhelming majority of children attend public schools, private schools have little political constituency to assist in gaining tax dollars." (Emphasis added.)

In addition, there is the steadily growing power of teachers' unions fiercely committed to making sure that not a cent of public money leaves the public schools. In more and more states, these unions are becoming increasingly proficient lobbyists, and the stronger they get, the less chance there is that any tax money is going to be allocated to shore up experimental learning "models" outside the public schools.

So if you want to start where the child is, after all the trumpeting auguries of the 1960s, he's still right there in the public schools. For the parents of 90 percent of the nation's schoolchildren, any meaningful transformation of schooling has to take place *there,* against the odds. And it can happen there, as is evident in Martin Schor's elementary school, and in schools explored in the pages to come.

Yet how substantive can these changes be? There is the argument by various radical education critics that until there is democratic socialism in the land, liberal school reform essentially amounts to tinkering with a system that is as exploitative and dehumanizing as the larger capitalist society of which the schools are an integral part.

Meanwhile, what of the millions of children in the schools who are learning right now that they are inferior material while, on the outside, these brave radicals (as they also pursue tenure) work to create a new socialist society for the trapped kids.

This, like the "free school" movement, is yet another way for some humanitarian, egalitarian adults to profess deeply abiding concern for the mass of children in this country, whom they indeed see as a mass that can't be helped where it is, right now.

Martin Schor, however, with his crucial, diligently kept record books, sees individual children. As does Gloria Channon, a remarkably astute and resourceful teacher in the New York City public schools. It was she, in an article in *Urban Review* (when it was published by the now-defunct Center for Urban Education), who provided me with what was to be the central reason for my writing this book:

The children come to us in the upper grades firmly fixed in their negative self-images, that is, they think they are dumb. When you talk to them about this feeling, you find a deep chasm exists between their experiences of success and this confirmed faith in their own stupidity. Lucy, having made the leap from nonreader to fourth-grade level in one feverish, compulsive, splendid year, was trying to explain why she had not been able to do so in the seven years of school before this one: "I'm dumb." Lucy had no other negative self-images that one could see. She was warm and loving, she could fight boys on the street, she could assume leadership in petitioning for a sixth-grade field day, she could dance at parties and laugh —oh, how she could laugh at the world and at herself! But the schools had given her seven years in which to learn that she was "dumb." She had accepted that terrible self-knowledge with grace and resignation. She had learned what math she could without reading. She had listened and looked, learning with her eyes and ears what books could not tell her. When finally she met, in this school, teachers who could give her what *she* needed to make the leap into reading—and that included faith and patience—then she could do it; she could, in this protected place, take a chance on being dumb, and take a chance on not being dumb after all. But no one had told her that it was the schools that had failed her. Always she had assumed the total responsibility for her failure.

Lucy is legion in our schools. And indeed the failure is not hers. To make it possible for more children like Lucy to realize that they are not dumb is why the principals and teachers in this book are in the schools, whatever their political ideologies, if they have any. To awaken a Lucy to her intelligence may not help quicken the Socialist Coming, unless she turns out to be a latter-day Emma Goldman. But to save a Lucy from believing herself dumb is a most valuable achievement all in itself.

Sometimes, however, to cast out dumbness it is necessary to turn a whole school around.

In April 1970, Luther Seabrook took over as principal of the William O'Shea Intermediate School (I.S. 44) at Amsterdam Avenue and 77th Street on Manhattan's West Side. At the time, I.S. 44 was far from the most enviable education berth in the city.

"Kids were roaming the halls," a veteran I.S. 44 teacher told me, "and there were days when it wasn't safe to go outside your classroom, let alone to the bathroom. One day, in fact, the tactical patrol force had to be called to protect some of the teachers from kids bombarding them with eggs. The funny thing is the kids really hit the right teachers with those eggs, but still . . . Anyway, that was by no means the only time the police showed up in those years. There were a lot of drugs around, and muggings were going on right inside the school.

"As for learning," the teacher continued, "the white kids in the special progress classes were doing O.K.; but in the other tracks, the black kids had never been respected, and nobody paid *any* attention to the Spanish-speaking kids. Leadership? For about eleven years we had a very angry man as principal —screaming at people, and once in a while bashing kids against the wall. I'm not kidding. I thought this school had no way to go but to the very bottom, and we were almost there."

The new principal had a preliminary idea of what he was getting into. Luther Seabrook, a black former teacher in the New York City school system, had just spent two years in Roxbury, a black section of Boston. (When I had gone to school there, it was a Jewish section of Boston.) In Roxbury, Seabrook had helped form and was the first principal of the independent, community-controlled Highland Park Free School. "I had finished laying the foundation for that," Seabrook said to me in his large, uncluttered office on the first floor of I.S. 44, "and I was looking for something new. I came down from Boston for an interview here. It was about ten o'clock in the morning, and as the cab turned the corner, I thought that, for some reason, school must be out. There were kids all over the street, and since all of them were either black or looked to be Hispanic, I figured to myself that this must be a totally Third World school." ("Third World" is a term favored by Seabrook to describe people or institutions that are not white.)

"Once I got inside the school," Seabrook—a lithe, informal man in his late forties, with an easy laugh but a continually watchful air—went on, "I found that there *were* kids in the classrooms, but most of them were white. I stayed around a couple of hours and saw that kids were just flowing in and out of the building—Third World kids with nothing to do. It was sort of an open classroom, you might say," Seabrook said caustically. "There was no system of accountability at all—for the teachers or for the kids. I saw about four or five fights while I was here, both in and outside the classrooms, and I figured, 'Man, you'd be crazy to take this job.' Besides, I also had a chance, at that time, to become principal of an elementary school on the West Side, and at the gut level, I feel it's in those first grades that turning the schools around really has to start. But I couldn't get myself to walk away from what was going on here. I said to myself, 'Nothing's impossible, right?' " Seabrook laughed. "So I decided to try I.S. 44."

On his first day as principal, Seabrook was soon faced with a disciplinary problem. A dean brought two boys, about twelve or thirteen, into the principal's office—a tall, hefty white youngster and a considerably smaller black member of the student body. The latter was charged with having mugged the white boy in the corridor.

"Did you mug him?" Seabrook asked the black boy.

"No, I asked him for a dime and he give it to me."

"Is that true?" Seabrook turned to the white boy.

"Yuh. But if I didn't give it to him, he would have beat me up or cut me with his knife or got his friends to beat me up."

The principal decided to hold a hearing, with both youngsters and their parents present. "I wanted to suggest to the boys' parents that both those kids were victims. I knew what racism had done to the black kid by what he was doing. And the white kid was also a victim of racism in that he saw the black youngster as being all-powerful, as being capable of doing whatever he wanted to with him."

At the hearing, the white student's father told Seabrook he had instructed his son not to resist if anyone asked him for money. Giving up some change, the father said, is vastly preferable to being hurt.

"I understand that," Seabrook said to the father, "but I have a problem with it. What's going to happen is that your son is going to give up nickels and dimes whenever something like this happens, and then he'll leave this school and go to Bronx Science or some other prestigious high school. From there he'll go on to Harvard or Yale and eventually, let's say, to Washington, where he'll be in a position to pass laws or make rules that will oppress this kid because all your son knows about this kid is that once, or more than once, he's shaken him down for some money.

"Now," Seabrook went on, gesturing toward the black youngster, "what do you think is going to happen to *this* kid? He'll get a dime from your son, a quarter from somebody else, a dollar from another boy, and then he's going to start getting five dollars from the guy at the newsstand at the corner and later, a hundred dollars from the grocery store. So where is he going to end up? At the University of Attica. Well, I'm not going to let these two kids do that to each other."

At that point, the black student's mother rose angrily from her chair, shouting at Seabrook, "How *dare* you say my son is going to prison?"

"I had walked right into that one," Seabrook told me, ruing the occasion. "I had not done my homework. I had just assumed that the black parent was on the same wavelength as I was. I mean, I had been active in Harlem CORE [the Congress of Racial Equality] and I had worked for civil rights in Mississippi. I thought everyone knew that about me. But that boy's mother saw me as just another nigger taking care of the man's business. Wow, that was a new kind of thing for me to experience, and it got through to me—hard."

Seabrook took the mother out into the hall and tried to explain what he was trying to do. She was too agitated to listen. "From then on," Seabrook says, "whenever a situation like this came up, I met with the black parents first and told them what I had in mind."

As for the aftermath to that particular incident, Seabrook met privately with the black youngster and told him, "Would you believe that there's a judge, sitting in his long black robes, right now, with a list of names in front of him? Next to each name on that list is a cell number at Attica or Elmira or some other prison. *Your* name is on that list. And would you believe that the system has you so programed that you're going to have to work like hell to get off that list?"

The black student began to laugh, but stopped when he saw Seabrook was dead serious. The principal and the boy had a number of talks after that. "I don't know if he really *believed* what I was saying," Seabrook says, "but something got through because he didn't get into any trouble after that. I also told that kid, 'The door to my office is always open, you hear me? You want a nickel, a dime, a quarter, you come *here* to get it.'

"Of course," Seabrook said to me, "the money wasn't at the root of it. Fear was. The white kid's fear, also the fear of the black kid that he wasn't going anywhere, so it didn't matter what he did. I've run down the whole thing—the judge in his black robes with his list of names—so often at this place that by now the kids really understand what I'm talking about."

During Seabrook's stay as principal, in any case, I.S. 44 changed markedly. Children no longer congregate outside in the street during school hours, and inside the three-story white brick building, faculty and students appear, for the most part, to be purposefully at work. There are still occasional disciplinary problems (and a school ombudsman to help handle them), as well as clashes, from time to time, between individual teachers and the principal over questions of educational policy. But clearly, I.S. 44 has been turned around.

Carol Lotz, a tall, immensely energetic woman, who inaugurated the school's Open Classroom Program in her own sixth-grade class in 1970 and has since expanded it to include some 190 sixth-, seventh-, and eighth-grade students, does not always agree with Seabrook on school matters, but gives him high grades for changing the spirit of the school. "Luther has created a feeling in the kids," she says, "that this is their school and that they have every right to complain to him if they feel they're getting a bad deal from anyone. His office really is open to them. Actually, sometimes it gets to where there's no point sending a kid to Luther for discipline. The kid would welcome the trip. But Luther is also open to us. Luther is the kind of principal who'll back you up if you want to try something new with the kids. That is, he'll back you up so long as you succeed. He'll give you time, sometimes even a year, but if your approach doesn't work, he holds you accountable and you've got to reexamine what you've been doing."

Attached to a wall in the principal's office on the first floor of I.S. 44 is a sheet of paper proclaiming Luther Seabrook to be the recipient of "The Ambivalence Award." Signed by Carol Lotz and other members of the Open Classroom staff at the school, the proclamation memorializes "our love-hate relationship" with the principal while expressing gratitude to Seabrook for the "joy and reward" he has given the signers.

"Another school year," Carol Lotz told me, "I gave him another prize, 'The Male Chauvinist Award,' because he kept refusing to tell the shop teachers to mix boys and girls in their shop classes. Luther was balking because he didn't want to *force* any teacher to do what he didn't want to, but damn it, that kind of integration of classes is a state law now. Luther and I had one big battle over that one. We do have about one Donnybrook a year, during which we don't speak to each other for two weeks. This time, because I rallied some outside support for what I wanted, including a state senator whose kid goes to this school and who, for God's sake, introduced that law, Luther sent me a letter ordering me to cease and desist my lobbying or he'd fire me. Well, boys and girls finally *were* integrated in the shop classes, and I ignored Luther's letter. At the end of that school year in June, when I looked in my file, that letter to me from Luther wasn't there. He hadn't wanted a reprimand to be part of my file. I'm sure we're going to have other arguments, but as for what Luther has done to this place, just compare it with most of the other schools in this city. This school is alive! And while there are problems with some of the new programs he's encouraged, the difference between I.S. 44 before he came and I.S. 44 now is like the difference we all felt before Nixon resigned and after."

There are some twelve hundred students at I.S. 44—approximately 20 percent of them white, 27 percent black, and the rest mostly Hispanic along with Haitian, Dominican, and Asian children. The school's reputation has so changed that a number of white parents in the neighborhood, who had expected to send their children to private school, have instead enrolled them at I.S. 44. When Luther Seabrook applied in 1973 for the position of community superintendent of School District 3 (of which I.S. 44 is part), among many parents protesting the possibility of his departure were, as Seabrook puts it, "a lot of my middle-class constituency." Seabrook recalls that one parent telephoned him and said, "You can't leave. My kid's been at I.S. 44 for two years and you've saved me six thousand dollars because if you hadn't been there, that kid would be in private school."

Word of the turning around of I.S. 44 has gone beyond District 3. In the school now are children from Queens, Brooklyn, and even one from Staten Island. Students also come down from Harlem rather than attend the intermediate school nearest them. I asked Seabrook how it was possible to keep admitting children from outside District 3's lines.

He laughed. "The beautiful thing about school decentralization," Seabrook said, "is that the Board of Education just wants you to stay out of their hair. If you don't bug them, if you don't ask them for a ruling, they're not going to volunteer to give you one. Of course, once you start messing up, then the man is going to come in and tell you what to do. We don't mess up."

To get I.S. 44 to the point at which it began to be prized by parents, Seabrook, as one of his first priorities, worked to change the attitudes of some of the school's teachers and to get rid of those who could not or would not alter their conception of what a teacher's responsibility should be. "There was a large segment of the staff," Seabrook told me, "who really cared about the kids. But a lot of *them* were what's called 'liberal educators.' They had some kind of funny feeling about making certain demands on kids. They were reluctant to do it. Then there were conservative teachers—I hate this kind of labeling, but I'll use it for discussion purposes—who would demand that everyone behave absolutely correctly in class or else get the hell out. But what happened to the kids who got thrown out didn't seem to concern those teachers at all. And there were teachers who were just hustling off the kids. They were in the school to make a buck, and for no other reason.

"Since I've been here, however," Seabrook continued, "there has been a significant change among the teachers. For one thing, some are not as destructive as they used to be. And you know, even well-meaning teachers can be destructive at times. Unknowingly, they can provoke a confrontation with a kid."

As an illustration, Seabrook told me of a young teacher who had spent all her lunch periods working with children who needed help in their studies. "She really had a mouth on her," Seabrook said, "but by God, she was one of the best teachers we had in terms of demanding that the kids do their work. She eventually left to have a child, but shortly before that, she got angry at a boy in her class and yelled at him, 'That's why you're so *stupid*—you never pay attention.' There are other ways of getting kids to pay attention, you hear me? Other ways than calling them stupid before the whole class. She picked a way—well, you know what came right back. The kid said something about her being a white bitch, among a good many other unpleasant things."

The teacher came to Seabrook and demanded that the boy be suspended for five days. The principal suggested that while the child should perhaps get a five-day suspension for overreaction, he also wondered whether the teacher herself ought not to get a three-day suspension for provoking that overreaction. As it happened, she and the boy worked their problem out, and nobody was suspended.

"That's Luther's way," another teacher told me. "When there's a conflict between two teachers or between a teacher and a kid, he hears them both out, comes up with some suggestions usually indicating neither is entirely right, and then lets them settle it themselves. If he sees that isn't about to happen, he'll step in."

With regard to the boy who swore at the teacher, Seabrook maintains that the incident need not have happened. "It's a question of sensitivity," he says. "And it's not only a matter of knowing how to talk to kids. You have to be attuned to the different value systems of different classes, different cultures. Take those kids who sometimes wear hats in this school. Clearly that first came from the Spanish kids, though more black kids are doing it now. We've had teachers getting very uptight about kids having hats on in class, but some of those same teachers don't get nearly so upset when white kids show up wearing patched-up blue jeans because in those teachers' value system, that's O.K., that's out of what used to be called the hippie subculture. It's something they understand. I'll tell you, so far as I'm concerned, I'm glad some of those kids with their hats on are *in* school. That's what counts.

"Anyway," Seabrook continued, "dealing with a clash of value systems, dealing with teachers' insensitivity to that and to other things is something I have to be on top of all the time. I have to be able to see it, explain it, and work with teachers on it. And I work in different ways with different teachers. Some are sharp enough so that all I have to do is lay it out and walk away. They pick right up on it. Others have to be worked with more, and some you can't do a damn thing about. Not only with regard to their 'sensitivity,' but what's obviously more important, with regard to their habit of failing to be able to teach the kids here. A lot of *those* teachers are no longer in this school."

I asked Seabrook how he had been able to get rid of teachers he didn't want in the school in view of the strong contract between the United Federation of Teachers and the Board of Education, a contract that makes it exceedingly difficult to dismiss a teacher.

"One thing you do," Seabrook answered, "is you start keeping a book on them, and you let them know that's what you're doing. Nothing sly. Nothing dirty. And finally you say, 'I think you'll be happier somewhere else. I want you to transfer out, and I'll help you find a spot.' That way of removing teachers is nothing new. It's the easiest way. Principals have been transferring teachers out for a long time. Another way, and I've used it, is to abolish a whole department in order to get rid of certain people. When I came here, there was a vocal music department with six or seven people in it. I wanted some of them out of the school, so I got rid of the whole department. Those I wanted to keep, I found other places for. And there are still other ways of freeing a school of teachers who aren't producing. You start putting pressure on a guy to make certain kinds of changes and you know damn well he's not going to make them so you keep the pressure on, keep the pressure on, keep the pressure on, until you finally tell the community superintendent, 'Look, we got to get this guy out of here or all hell will break loose.' I've used that way, too. After all, if a principal gives a damn about his school, it's up to him to decide who ought to teach in it. And let's face it, if a principal really wants to get rid of someone, he can do it. There's no question about that.

"Now, that does not mean"—Seabrook rose from his desk—"that I give a damn about what kind of method a teacher uses. I'm willing to let anyone try anything, so long as they give me back the results I want. If you're teaching reading, I don't care if you use phonics or look-say. You find a way that's comfortable for you, and do it. If you don't do it so that it works, you had better find another way that does work, or get out, because I will not let any teacher keep screwing up kids."

During one of my visits to I.S. 44, I looked in on the Open Classroom Program, which several seasoned administrators of that form of learning had told me was one of the best in the city. In one of the reports that flow regularly to parents from each of the school's programs—there is also, since Luther Seabrook came, a large, comprehensive school-wide report sent to parents each June—Carol Lotz had pointed out that the Open Classroom Program "is the only British Infant System adaptation currently operating in the *secondary* schools of New York City." She went on to explain:

> Open Classroom simply means that each subject is taught by presenting a variety of activities and experiences that the student can choose from according to his abilities and interests. The teacher is "open" to the needs of each student, helping them to discover what skills they need to develop and providing different ways for them to learn. Each student is "graded" according to his progress and effort and competes only with himself. Detailed records are kept on the work they have completed, and conferences between the student and the teachers help them to understand what skills they need to develop and their individual goals for learning. Parents are fully informed of the student's progress and needs at conferences and with detailed quarterly reports.

Having visited a good many open classroom and open corridor programs in various parts of the country, my initial criterion of how well they're working—because the kids usually seem to be having a good time, whether a program is sloppily or efficiently run—is to find out if the teachers actually do keep detailed records of the strengths and weaknesses of each child. I am, I confess, more interested, as my own children move through school, in academic strengths and weaknesses rather than in the "affective learning" benefits which open classroom partisans claim, usually correctly, to be a particular dividend of this approach to learning.

At I.S. 44, Carol Lotz and her colleagues do indeed keep thorough records and appear to know where each child is, in the achievement of various skills, and where he ought to be. What particularly impressed me was the note in I.S. 44's annual comprehensive school reports to parents, that "thirty-eight of our sixty-four graduates [eighth-graders in the Open School Program] passed the tests for the special high schools."

Since most of the children in that graduating class had been in the program for three years, clearly a considerable amount of learning had been going on. The community served by I.S. 44 seems to agree, since there are always considerably more applicants than vacancies in I.S. 44's Open School Program.

Stepping over a child stretched out in the corridor, reading, I walked into Carol Lotz's office and saw a notice on the wall:

The Policy of This Office

Adults have the right to blow their stacks, gripe, be in bad moods, be silly, be busy, and generally be human.

Kids have the right to ask questions, complain, interrupt, share problems, show their work, and generally be human.

No one has the right to be rude or harsh, make a mess, be too noisy or be unfair to anyone.

Carol Lotz looked up from a sheaf of papers as I read the notice. "Open classroom," she said, "means open for the teacher, too. I mainly put that up so it would be in writing that I have the right to blow my stack."

Downstairs, on a bulletin board in a first-floor corridor, there was a drawing I hadn't seen before. It was of a classroom, with three students reading. On top, the artist, an eighth-grade Puerto Rican boy, had printed: "YOUR ENGLISH IS SHOWING." Underneath the drawing was a warning: "All your life you will be judged on your basic English skills: speaking, writing, reading." Next to the sketch was a photograph of a dance class. Under it someone had crayoned: "1972–74, Major Dance."

On another bulletin board nearby was a drawing of a young man dejectedly leaving an industrial plant. A guard looked at him disdainfully. This drawing was captioned: "Big deal: So I was five minutes late."

In the principal's office, I waited as Luther Seabrook gave

two girls carfare for a trip to the Bronx High School of Science, where they were to take entrance examinations. He also quizzed them to be sure they knew how to get to the school. Looking at the variety of posters and clippings on the principal's wall, I was held by a printed credo:

Telling lies to the young is wrong.

Proving to them that lies are true is wrong.

Telling them God's in his heaven and all's right with the world is wrong.

The young know what you mean.

The young are people.

One of those people, a short, slight white boy who looked to be about fourteen walked into the principal's office to say good-bye to Seabrook. The boy's father, an expert in administering welfare programs, had a new job in Atlanta.

"Hey," Seabrook said to me as the boy came in and the two girls bound for Bronx Science left, "I want you to meet this character." The boy and I shook hands. "I have a story about this young man when he was here," Seabrook said. "Some guy, a big guy, went up to him and asked him for a quarter. So this character"—Seabrook laughed—"said to him, 'Are you kid-ding?' This character was a hick at the time; he hadn't gotten hip yet. And you know what the big guy said?" Seabrook was laughing so hard he couldn't continue for a moment. "He said, 'Aw, I was only asking.'"

"There's a better story about my sister," the white boy said. "She was at the water fountain on the third floor, and this guy comes up to her and says, 'Gimme your money.' She says, 'No! Gimme *yours!*' *And he pulls out his money!*" Seabrook roared again. "My sister," the boy continued, "she just dropped his money on the floor. She didn't know what to do with it."

Seabrook and the boy talked for a while about the schools in Atlanta and then the boy started out of the room, looked back, and waved cheerfully at the principal, who waved back.

"I'm sorry to see that kid go," Seabrook told me. "Of course, that kid is programed so he'll make it anywhere. As would most of the middle-class kids in this school. My job is to see to it that *all* the kids here feel there's a reason for their going on. Take the Open Classroom Program on the third floor. I think it's an excellent way to educate kids. I think that in my head; but I know in my gut that if my child were in that program, I would monitor her very closely. If you're part of the Third World, you can't afford the luxury of a child of yours going through that kind of thing and not getting enough out of it. And when it comes to college, for another example, I don't think we can afford liberal arts majors either. I had a big fight about that with my oldest daughter. She was majoring in liberal arts at Howard, and it cost me a Volkswagen to get her to change her mind. I gave her the car and she changed her major to communications. At this point in our family's development, we need people with particular skills."

I brought the conversation back to the Open Classroom Program because I was curious about the fact that, despite Seabrook's ambivalences toward it, the program had expanded during his leadership of the school. I asked him how integrated the program was.

"There are a lot of middle-class kids in it," he said. "Actually that program is one of the reasons white parents keep their kids here. But I don't allow it to get anything extra from the school. If anything, that program gets a little less in terms of resources. And my input up there is pretty negligible. I've got a bigger job to do in the rest of the school. On the other hand, no Third World kid who has ever wanted to go into the Open Classroom Program has ever been denied the right to. I really do believe in choices and alternatives. I don't believe in locking people into anything. But to tell you the truth, it wouldn't bother me if the Open Classroom Program consisted entirely of white middle-class kids—so long as the children in it don't act and are not perceived by the other kids in the school as being superior. I'd rather have the program be as integrated as possible, but there are a lot of other things going on in this school besides open classrooms."

A short, chubby sixth-grader appeared at the door and asked the principal if her English teacher was inside.

"No, sweetheart," Seabrook said. "He's in the lunchroom."

The principal turned back to me. "I'll tell you something else about this school. No kid is allowed to graduate with less than a 6.2 reading score. *No kid!* That's the minimum score a kid needs to get into the academic track in high school. Otherwise he's 'promoted' into the goddamn general track. That's part of what I've been fighting for years. The public schools have been created by and designed for the white middle class. They don't serve Third World kids, and they don't serve poor whites either. What happens, therefore, is that youngsters who have no guarantees in this system are allowed to just keep slipping through until they finally slip out of the whole damn school system because they know that for them there's no prize at the end of the rainbow. That's why I've been fighting to have strict promotional guidelines in *all* schools in this district."

I asked Seabrook about a ruling a while ago by Irving Anker, chancellor of the New York public school system, that children could no longer be automatically promoted.

"That's not quite what he said," Seabrook answered. "The net effect of his ruling is that a child can get held back only once in elementary school and only once in the secondary schools. So they'll *still* slip through, and many eventually will slip out. Obviously, where you should start preventing their slipping out is in the first, second, and third grades. Youngsters who don't achieve there should be held back, regardless of how many times it's necessary—*provided that* the teachers are really trying to get them to learn and *provided that* those teachers are continually monitored so you can be sure the kids are getting strong academic input.

"But let me show you what actually happens." Seabrook took a Manila folder out of a desk drawer. "Look at these reading scores. These are kids who came here in the sixth grade this year from elementary schools in this district." He ran his finger down a list of scores. "One hundred sixty-six kids from this elementary school came here reading below 4.5. Look at the scores from the next school. Again, most of them below 4.5. And look at all the kids reading on a second-grade level. Twos, twos, twos." He moved his finger down the list, his voice sounding as if it were intoning a grim litany. "Look at that—1.8!"

There had been a time, earlier in Seabrook's stay as principal of I.S. 44, when he had called to his office the principals of four elementary schools feeding into I.S. 44. "I tried to work out some kind of connection between their schools and ours, besides just moving the children along. What I really wanted was to try to have some influence on what they're doing in their schools."

"Did you have any impact on them?" I asked.

Seabrook shook his head. "No. They respond only to real power, and I don't have any real power over them. Of course, they're sophisticated enough by now not to tell me explicitly that they're dealing with 'poor' material. They just say, 'We're doing the best we can.' And so we get sixth-graders with scores like these. It's lack of accountability again. Principals are not doing what they get paid for, teachers are not doing what they get paid for, and yet these educational *professionals* complain about lack of public support for the schools.

"Meanwhile," Seabrook said, "at least I have my own little piece of turf here, and I'm going to keep it clean of people who aren't doing their jobs. If I had the district, I would keep the district clean; and if I had the city, I'd keep the city clean. But at this point, the only power I have is here. And I use it to push everything that happens in this school toward accountability.

For instance, I test all kids who are reading below their grade level four times a year. One reason is so that the kids can see some progression in terms of what they're doing. And the reading scores here, by and large, are going up. But second, those tests enable me to focus in on teachers whose kids aren't moving up. I show them the scores and tell them, 'Hey, let's find out where the problem is and do something about it.' "

One of the programs at I.S. 44 that Seabrook monitors most closely is the Reading Power Commune, which he instituted a year and a half after he became principal. The commune is a diagnostic and prescriptive reading-development center involving some 175 children who read at least two years below grade level, with some reading as many as six years below grade level. "There's no point euphemizing," Seabrook says. "There are many functional illiterates in that program." Through diverse tests, the particular deficiencies of a child—in decoding words, phonics, reading comprehension, or in all three—are identified. Based on individual diagnoses, a specific remedial program is prescribed for each child. Among other elements of the Reading Power Commune are intensive reading periods, some of which involve programed instruction through machines. Where special help is needed, individual tutoring is provided, and on occasion, two children are paired so that they can help each other.

"We use every kind of approach we can think of," a coordinator of the Reading Power Commune says. "For some kids, sheet music works. They want to learn to read the lyrics of their favorite songs. Some teachers have used the sports pages of the *Daily News* with considerable success. In one class, a kid came into the program with a reading score of 2.7. In seven months, partly because of his passion for the New York Knicks, about whom he read avidly in the *Daily News,* he was reading at a 4.1 level. In the process, by the way, he also made a Knick fan of his teacher."

"Whatever works, we'll use," a teacher in the Reading Power

Commune told me. "The idea is not to keep these kids in the commune throughout their time in this school, but to get their reading ability to the point at which they can rejoin the mainstream of the other students. It can be a long climb for some of the kids, but scores do go up, and if we keep at it, I think we can eventually get most of the kids who are way behind when they come into the school up to grade level by the time they leave.

"It may not sound exciting to you," the teacher said, "but it's a marvelous feeling of triumph when a kid who could just barely read when he started in September announces that now he can read everything on a cereal box. Another kid, who I don't think had ever read a book in his life, got through all of *Robinson Crusoe* last term. And once in a while, there's a dramatic leap. Last year a Puerto Rican girl raised her score from 2.0 to 5.1. Can you imagine what that means to a kid—*to know you're not really dumb, after all!* Damn it, there's no reason why she should have fallen so far behind by the time she came here. We're doing for these kids what their elementary school teachers should have done six years ago."

The presence of the Reading Power Commune, along with other continually evaluated remedial programs, also appears to explain in part the decline of disciplinary problems at I.S. 44. "If a kid feels embarrassed," a tutor told me, "because he can't read and because that failure cuts him off from the rest of the school, he's likely to get out his frustrations by raising hell. This way, he feels he's accomplishing something, and so he puts his energy into trying to accomplish even more."

"It's the damnedest thing," Carol Lotz says of the Reading Power Commune. "I do not believe in homogeneous classes. I do not believe in segregating kids from the rest of the school. I do not believe in programed materials. But those kids stay in those rooms, and they *like* it. I suppose it's because they don't feel threatened. They're not competing with kids reading way ahead of them. I do think some of the teachers they have there need a lot more training, but they obviously care about the kids, and that gets through, too."

For some 120 Puerto Rican, Dominican, and Haitian children who come from homes in which Spanish or French is the primary and sometimes the only language spoken, there is a bilingual (actually a trilingual) program at I.S. 44. The program focuses on intensive instruction in English as a second language while also stressing the study of the child's native language and including a bilingual approach to math, science, social studies, and other subjects.

"Instead of just throwing these kids into the general student body, where they'd be made to feel alien to the school," a teacher in the bilingual program told me forcefully, "we give them a chance to acquire some self-confidence, to discover they can learn in a school system where at first they felt like utter strangers. It took all these years and a long court suit before finally a federal court judge ordered bilingual education in all schools in this city for Hispanic kids who have so much difficulty with English that they keep falling back in everything. This school didn't wait for a court order. You know, I don't understand the resistance among some people in education to bilingual education. It's just plain common sense. Of course, to have as many bilingual teachers as this city needs is going to require a lot of licensed teachers themselves to become proficient in a second language. So I guess I do understand some of that long-term resistance.

"Thank God," she said, "Seabrook understands why it's so necessary. But he doesn't give us all the support we need. We need at least another class, another teacher, and a guidance counselor. It's almost criminal to scrimp and save on kids who have to learn how to adapt to a whole other culture."

One morning, after spending some time in a bilingual class in social studies, I was walking toward one of the rooms in the Reading Power Commune and saw, in bold letters, on a sign attached to the wall:

READ NOW, NOT TOMORROW.
TOMORROW MAY BE TOO LATE.

The principal, who was walking alongside me, pointed to the sign. "The question is," he said, "how do you get a poor reader to do anything about that? If he can read that sign to begin with. There's no question in my mind that reading is the key to freedom. I don't think anybody can be free unless he can read. But one of the things I did when I first came to I.S. 44 was to start destroying reading as the *only* symbol of success in school. Now hear me, there is no contradiction between those two positions."

I was dubious. "What about the Reading Power Commune?" I asked.

"That's not the only way we teach reading here," Seabrook said. "Let me explain what I mean. You're middle class. I'm middle class. I know that my kid goes to school with the ability to read, or certainly being ready to read. I see to that. Now, Mary Jones doesn't do that at home. Her kid and my kid come into the first grade. Both can be equally bright. But my kid, because she jumps ahead in reading, gets put into one group—let's say, the Blue Jays—and Mary Jones's kid is placed in another group with another name. But the kids know what those names mean. They mean the smart class and the dumb class. As Kenneth Clark says, decisions are made in the first grade that can affect youngsters for the rest of their lives.

"If I were running an elementary school," Seabrook continued, "I would have other symbols of success in addition to reading. Music, drama, art—there are a number of areas in which kids could achieve, could feel positive about themselves. I am in no way saying that reading should be neglected with those kids. Mary Jones's kid has *got* to learn to read, and read well. But with these other success options going for him, he won't feel that if other kids are ahead of him in reading at some given point, he's dumb all around.

"O.K.," Seabrook said, "I don't have an elementary school. But what I have done here, in a junior high school, is to add to the things kids can major in. When I came, they had art majors and music majors. We brought in science majors, dance majors, health education majors, math majors, aviation majors—different ways to make a kid feel he can succeed in subjects other than reading. At the same time, whatever the major is, reading is basic to everything we do. But it's not the *only* immediate way to feel good about yourself, to know that you can achieve."

"Tell me," I said. "You're achieving here as a principal, and I've been in other schools where the principals, although they do things differently than you do, also insist that the kids learn and make sure they do learn. But what about all the others? How can parents make *all* principals earn their salaries?"

"It's got to start," Seabrook said, "with there being enough parents in a school who actually believe they have the power to make principals accountable. I'm thinking particularly of Third World parents. Some are making themselves heard, but there are a lot of others—and this is a horrible thing for me to have to recognize—who do not believe their kids can learn. They really don't believe it. And that's an effect of racism. Take the Third World parents in this school. I think that by now they trust us; they *are* seeing their kids can learn. But I have a sense that some of them feel their kid is the lucky exception. I hate to tell you this, but that's the way I felt about myself when I was a kid. I was damn near an adult before I realized that all white people weren't extra-smart, super-smart, in comparison to us. I'm serious, you hear me."

Luther Seabrook was born and grew up in Charleston, South Carolina. His family, as he puts it, was "typically upper-lower class." His father worked two jobs—a janitor by day and a bartender at night. His mother, a product of the Catholic schools in Charleston, ran a summer school for her own children so that they would be well prepared for the private schools they attended at various stages of their education.

"Schooling was *very* important in our family," Seabrook recalls, "and that notion stuck. In addition to me, three of my sisters are teachers. They went to Avery Institute in Charleston, which was run by the American Missionary Association of the Congregational Churches of America. I went to public elementary school, but when it came to high school, my mother and father insisted I go to Lincoln Academy in Kings Mountain, North Carolina. That was also run by the American Missionary Association."

Lincoln Academy, no longer in existence, had an all-black student body, and an index of the accountability it demanded of its students was the rule that no one could remain on any of the school's athletic teams if he did not maintain a B average in his studies. Black history and culture were included in the rigorous curriculum. "We used such books," Seabrook says, "as Sylvester C. Watkins's *Anthology of American Negro Literature* and Carter Woodson's *The Negro in Our History.* We were into black culture before it became modish. And in nearly everything we studied, the emphasis was analytic, not just memorization of facts. Like a marvelous course which examined the Civil War from the perspective of the South as well as of the North."

At Lincoln Academy, the firm expectation was that every graduate would go on to college. "It never entered our minds," Seabrook remembers, "that there was any alternative. You hear that? Now that's positive programing. On the other hand, we were not programed to attend only black colleges. The kids from Lincoln Academy went to any school they wanted to—if they had the grades."

Seabrook, however, went to West Virginia State, near Charleston, West Virginia. Almost entirely black at the time, the college was primarily a teacher-training institution. "I didn't feel any overwhelming call to teach," Seabrook says, "but there weren't that many other options. An uncle of mine, for instance, is a graduate of South Carolina State College, and he recently retired from the post office. You follow me? If you didn't want to go that kind of route, your choices were to teach, preach, or, if you were extremely lucky and your parents could afford it, you could try to go to medical school."

After two years at West Virginia State, Seabrook served in the Air Force from 1948 to 1952, working on the ground in supplies, in aviation engineering, and for a brief period, in the air police. "I couldn't swing that last one," Seabrook says with a laugh. "I just don't have the mentality that kind of job requires." Following his discharge from the Air Force, Seabrook returned for a year and a half to West Virginia State, from which he was graduated with a bachelor of science in education. For his master's degree, he came to New York to attend Columbia University's Teachers College while simultaneously working full-time at a juvenile detention center on the Lower East Side. It was, as I recall, considered a very rough place to work in, but Seabrook says he had no problems with any of his charges.

"I never have problems with kids, man," he told me. "Why? I can tell you something corny like I respect them, and it's true. And they've always been able to trust me. I have never played any games with kids. I don't jive them. If I tell them I'm going to do something, I do it, but I always tell them first. I don't spring things on them."

Seabrook liked the work at the detention center, but he did not enjoy his year at Teachers College, where he received his master's degree in health education. "There was only one guy on the faculty I felt I could talk to," Seabrook says. "Some of them seemed to feel I should be very grateful for having been allowed to come to Teachers College. And there were others— well, let me tell you my problem with people teaching me. If I had a choice of instructors, give me someone who is hard and straight and—I hate to use the term—treats everyone alike. I can deal with that. I did not like the teachers I had who were patronizing nor did I like those on the other side who didn't think I could do the work. Maybe I look for trouble, but in any case, Teachers College was not a good experience for me."

After getting his degree, Seabrook left New York for two years of teaching and coaching basketball at a black Baptist school, Florida N & I (Normal and Industrial) College in St. Augustine. "Those were two good years," Seabrook recalls. "Teaching there was real missionary work, and I admired the staff of a school like that. They would grab kids, really glorified high school kids, where they were and try like hell to bring them up to where they should be. I used to see teachers take kids and spend hours walking and talking with them."

In 1957, Seabrook was back in New York, teaching health education at a junior high school in East Harlem, where he volunteered to take over the C.R.M.D. (Children with Retarded Mental Development) class. "There had been three teachers in two weeks in that class," he says. "I had no experience in teaching mentally retarded youngsters, but I liked those kids. They were good kids. In gym, I got them into things they could really excel at—tumbling, basketball, that kind of stuff."

On Saturdays, and sometimes on Sundays as well, Seabrook would meet the kids he taught, along with their friends, in Central Park, where they would play ball. There were also occasional visits to museums. "One of them, the Museum of Natural History," Seabrook says, "we never did go into. It was a Saturday and we had planned to spend the whole day at that museum. But when we got there, the first thing we saw was that goddamn statue in front. Teddy Roosevelt on a horse; walking behind him a native American, half naked, his head down; and on the other side, a black man, also with his head down, and damn near naked. The kids and I just sat out there and we had a long lesson in the symbols of racism. You know,

I never have gone inside that museum. I understand it's a
fantastic place, but I don't give a damn what's in it so long as
that statue's there. Anyway, my class and I began looking
around the city for other symbols of racism. They're not hard
to find. Have you ever seen that statue in Beecher Park in
Brooklyn? There's Henry Ward Beecher reading the Bible, and
at his feet, two blacks, kneeling.

"There was no lack of lucidity among those allegedly retarded kids when we talked about such things as symbols of
racism," Seabrook continued. "For that matter, once those
C.R.M.D. kids were on the basketball court, they knew all the
rules. And they knew exactly what their favorite basketball
player's average was at the time, how many points he had
scored the night before, that sort of thing. It was remarkable
to watch how they picked up information. Those C.R.M.D. kids
had capacity, real capacity, which could have been built on. No
question about it. But I wasn't enough into myself at the time
to be of real help to them. Most of what I did for them was
social. I did keep telling them that if you can talk, you can read,
that there's nothing mysterious about reading, that it ain't so
big a thing to learn how to do. But very few of them did begin
to read. I didn't know enough then about reaching people to get
those kids to begin to realize their capacities."

Luther Seabrook feels that a turning point in his life, an
experience that enabled him to become a much better teacher,
was his participation in the Mississippi Summer of 1964. An
active member of Harlem CORE, Seabrook had attended
CORE's national convention in Kansas City in June of that
year. "The guy who was heading one of CORE's projects in
Mississippi spoke to us about what was happening there," Seabrook recalls, "and we just started crying. I said to myself, 'Why
the hell am I going back to New York? Mississippi is where I
ought to be.' So first I went down to Memphis for the SNCC
[Student Nonviolent Coordinating Committee] orientation
course; and then I was sent to Hattiesburg, Mississippi, where

I was asked to put together a freedom school at St. Paul's Church.

"It was in Mississippi," Seabrook says, "that I first became really sensitive to the class thing among blacks. I had always thought of class division in terms of only whites, never within the black community. I remember the first time I had to sit down at a meal, a guest of poor people down there, with flies all around, and hey, man, that was the hardest meal I ever got through. But you better believe I got through it. Being in Mississippi that summer taught me a lot. I learned to feel comfortable around really poor people. I learned to listen to *them* in rap sessions rather than just pay attention to middle-class people because they were more articulate."

When Seabrook returned to teaching in New York City in the fall of 1964, he began to get into more trouble than he ever had before in his teaching career. "It got to be," Seabrook says, "that any time there was a symbol of racism in school, I'd address myself to it. Like once the kids were being shown movies, and before the feature there was a cartoon about some droopy-eyed Black Sambo plodding along. All kinds of things happen to him, but even if the building falls on him, he doesn't care. I went up and made the guy running the machine take the cartoon off the goddamn reel. The assistant principal, a white guy with whom I had been close—we used to go to sports events together—ordered the projectionist to put the picture back on. He said I was just a teacher, that I didn't have the right to decide what was shown and what wasn't.

"I took my class right out of the auditorium. We all stood outside in the hall, and then I had a confrontation with the principal. I told him that this being a school, we were trying to prepare these kids for living in the future, and it seemed to me that whoever was responsible for the films that were shown in the school had to preview them and take out any that were racist. The principal sort of half agreed, but indicated that no one was really responsible for what had happened. I told him,

'Indeed, sir, *you* are responsible.' So the principal was on my back after that."

Seabrook got into further trouble with the school's administration by persuading all the black teachers, and some of the white ones, to join the parents' association. "We started having sessions with the parents," Seabrook says, "to point out to them some of the things they ought to be looking for in the school, things that they had the power to get done, like making the teachers and the principal accountable. The administration got *very* defensive about that, and although the principal never had the guts to tell me directly what a disruptive bastard he thought I was, he did finally say to me, when I left, 'You know, you're a tragedy. There's no way for you to move up in this system.' I knew exactly what he meant. Awhile before, I had been half offered a job there as acting assistant principal. By half offered, I mean the message was that I could have the job if I agreed to join their team and not make any more trouble. Well, I wasn't playing that game."

In 1966, Seabrook joined the Board of Education's human relations unit and was assigned to the Central Harlem School District. There Seabrook was often at odds with the district superintendent as well as with his own superiors at the Board of Education. One series of offenses was his helping parents get rid of the principals at several unachieving schools. After two years as part of the human relations unit, Seabrook, in the spring of 1968, was told by its director, a black man, that there was no longer a line for him in the unit's budget. "Luther," the human relations director said to him, "some of the things you do have to be done, but why must it be *you* doing them all the time? You get labeled as a troublemaker, Luther, and that can kill you."

For some time before, Seabrook had been in contact with a group of black parents in Boston who were trying to set up their own school outside the public school system, which they strongly and justifiedly felt had been disastrous for their children. Simultaneously, Seabrook had been trying to convince New York City's educational hierarchy to act on a proposal he had written. "The title was 'An Approach to Education in the Ghetto,'" Seabrook recalls. "My starting point was the so-called 'disruptive child.' I was saying, O.K., teachers are telling me that if they could get rid of disruptive Johnny, they'd have a beautiful class. But in my gut I know that if they're given the power to throw out Johnny because they've labeled him 'disruptive,' next year they'll get rid of Harry and Joe—and finally the teachers will be there all by themselves. My idea was to take a place, put all the Johnnys in it, and have it stay open twenty-four hours a day. It would be a place where kids could study, could meet after school, could spend the night if they had to. It would also be a place where parents could come, meet with the teachers, and meet with the kids, all the kids. In sum, it would be a community school. The idea was getting nowhere with the Board of Education here and so, because these Boston parents were interested in starting a community school, something like the one I had planned, I went to work in Boston."

By September 1968, the Highland Park Free School in Roxbury, with initial funding from the Ford Foundation, among other sources, was open. It began with 125 children, and its student population had grown to about 225 by the time Seabrook left the school in April 1970.

"One presupposition I had," Seabrook told me, "was that kids who had been untouched, or largely untouched, by the public school system as it was in Boston would not behave in school like some of the kids who had been blighted by it. That proved true. On the elementary level, that school in Roxbury was the most beautiful thing you'd ever want to see in terms of kids learning. But on the so-called junior high school level, dealing with kids who had already been turned off by the public schools, we caught absolute hell. With some kids, we had to work out deals. 'O.K., buddy,' I'd say to a kid who hadn't been in school for three or four years, 'you give me two hours a day, that's all I want from you.' Or with other kids, the deal would be, 'Hey, it's up to you when to come, but you've got to promise me that you'll work for forty-five minutes once you're here.' And it worked.

"Let me tell you about one of the most destructive kids we had. I'll never forget that little son of a bitch as long as I live. He was about thirteen when I first got to know him. He hadn't been to school for two years. His father was a trucker who used to take the boy along on his trips, and the kid wanted to stay with his father. He didn't want to have anything to do with school. The first day he was at Highland Park, this kid pulled a knife on a teacher. He expected to get kicked out, right? We didn't kick him out. Gradually the kid and I became friends. 'Didn't you hear about me pulling a knife on the teacher?' he asked me one day. I said I had. 'Why didn't you suspend me?' he said. 'Oh, is that what you wanted?' I told him. 'Why didn't you ask?'

"What I had done with the teacher involved," Seabrook told me, "was tell him the boy's background and ask him to cool it for a while. 'Let the boy get to know you,' I said, 'and then we'll see what happens.' Well, for the rest of that school year, the kid was absent only once. Oh, he did not become a model student right away, by any means. He waited six months to see if the school was going to adjust to him, and when he finally felt he could trust us, his reading score—from March to June—moved from 1.6 to 3.1, and his language-skill development score went from 1.6 to 4.3. The next year, we couldn't get rid of that kid. He wouldn't go home from school at three; he wouldn't go home at five. And by the end of that second year, his reading score had gone up to damn near 6.0. It wasn't that we had such remarkable reading teachers. What we had been able to do was to remove a lot of the factors—*like the fear of being considered dumb*—that had gotten in the way of his being able to learn."

Seabrook also emphasizes what parents learned about their own capacities at the Highland Park Free School. In an article,

"A New Experiment in Black Education," in the magazine *Social Policy,* Seabrook has pointed out:

> In setting up the school, parents made some interesting decisions, such as:
> 1. Seventy-five percent of the children must come from families earning less than $1,000 per family member a year.
> 2. Only children from the community would be accepted.
> 3. No tuition would be charged.
> 4. Only one middle-income parent could serve as a voting member of any standing committee.

> The parents have done some funny things, too. For instance, with a waiting list of over a hundred "qualified" youngsters, they went out and knocked on doors to recruit very poor youngsters. Many of the youngsters were not bringing nutritional lunches to school, so a hot-lunch program was implemented. Parents served as teachers one afternoon a month to free teachers to attend workshops. Parents were hired as teachers for the summer school *but only* those parents who had little or no involvement with the school. Funny people, Black parents.

> One parent who had come to me almost in tears because she was asked to go into a classroom, begging to be allowed to "sweep the floor," came up with a project to list all of the resources of the community within a booklet. She felt that folks should be sharing their resources with one another, as well as "keeping our money in the community." Her latest project was a family Halloween Party. Another parent had the initial idea for a proposal to start a catering service for the school and other community agencies. Four parents volunteered each day to prepare hot lunches for the staff and children. Funny people, Black parents.

Several years after he had left Roxbury to accept the post of principal of I.S. 44 in Manhattan, Seabrook emphasized that in helping start the Highland Park Free School, he had had two basic goals. "One was to have a place where black kids could learn. The other was to show the black parents of Roxbury that black kids can learn. We did both."

A black girl, about thirteen, in a black leather jacket, was crying outside the door of Luther Seabrook's office at I.S. 44 one morning as I came along the corridor.

"O.K.," the principal said to her, "now go wash your face."

"You going to tell my teacher something?" she asked.

"Yes," said Seabrook, "and later I'm going to tell you something."

She walked down the corridor, I went into the office, and about ten minutes later, as Seabrook and I were talking, the girl's young, bearded white teacher came in.

"Cynthia was here." Seabrook looked up at him. "What happened?"

"It's a long story," the teacher said. "You don't want to hear it."

"I've already heard her version," Seabrook said. "It was very simple. She was taking a test, you came in, told her to get up and get out. She got angry, tore up her test, you gave her a pass to leave the building, but she didn't want to leave the building, she wanted to go to her next class. She doesn't want to speak to you now, but she will speak to you after lunch."

"Did she mention to you," the teacher said, "that she was copying everything off the paper of the girl next to her? I told her I was going to move her to a room next door and she got very excited. Anyway, I know there are a few screws loose there to begin with."

"I hear something else," Seabrook said, "and it has nothing to do with any screws being loose. Of course she was dead wrong, and knowing that you knew she wasn't playing the game fairly made her embarrassed as hell. So how does a girl like Cynthia behave in that situation? The way she did behave. Look, she *does* want to talk to you after she gets control of herself, and I wish you would talk to her rather than leaving it like this."

The teacher shrugged. "O.K.," he said, "I'll talk to her after lunch. If it's productive, wonderful. If it's not, I'll talk to her mother." Moving past me as he went toward the door, the teacher mumbled, "I still think it's a waste of time." At the door, he turned around and said somewhat acidly to the principal, "Thanks, fearless leader, for your advice."

"I hear you, man," Seabrook called after him. "I hear you." The principal laughed. "He doesn't pick up all the signals yet. If a kid wants to talk to you after she's done something like that, it's important that you listen. Otherwise the whole thing will fester inside her. That's what makes our ombudsman so valuable. He knows how to listen."

The ombudsman of I.S. 44 is Steve Kaminsky, who is also the school's drug education specialist. I asked Seabrook how he had come to select Kaminsky.

"Steve wasn't my first choice," Seabrook said. "But let me tell you why I decided we needed an ombudsman. There was a dean here who used to come on like a cop. He's down in the lunchroom one day and he comes up to two guys, whose girl friends are also standing there. The dean sniffs the air and accuses both guys of smoking. There's no doubt in my mind he was right. They just ducked the cigarettes the second they saw him coming. O.K., one of them admits he was smoking. The other denies it. So the dean, after a few words, grabs the kid who said he wasn't smoking, finds a pack of cigarettes, and in front of all of them, he strips the cigarettes, one by one. You hear me?

"Now, this guy is being shamed in front of his girl friend. What's he going to do? What he did was come up here, kick the door in, and turn the office upside down. Obviously, I wasn't here at the time. Well, all hell broke loose. The dean demanded that the kid be suspended and that he pay for the door. I talked to the kid for a long time, and I don't think he's going to do anything like that again. But you know, that kind of confrontation wasn't necessary in the first place. There were other less inflammable ways in which the dean could have made his point.

"That incident got me to thinking," Seabrook said. "It was only one of a number of confrontations between kids and teachers that had been going on. I mean particularly confrontations that the teachers, unknowingly, had provoked. And the same kids were always involved, again and again. That was the horrible thing about it. So I decided we needed an ombudsman, someone the kids could go to and someone a teacher could call to help resolve a conflict before it blew up.

"Now, the guy I wanted for that job, a black guy, was a hero around here. The parents and the other teachers admired him a lot. He was also the most physical guy around here. He'd hit kids occasionally. Not maliciously, but he'd hit them. Yet there appeared to be no resentment against him among the kids. O.K., the school is mostly Third World, so it seemed to me that a black ombudsman was a logical choice. I dropped his name on the older kids as a possible choice for the job. *No way.* I had not been hip enough to recognize, until then, what they really thought of him. So I asked them their choice. Kaminsky, they said. He's not black, but they trust him.

"Come on." Seabrook got up from his desk. "Time to get out of here. I go around the classrooms once a day, often twice. It's the only way to know what's going on."

"Hey, Seabrook!" a short, round black youngster shouted at the principal as we went up the stairs to the second floor.

"Hey, fathead, how you doing?" Seabrook smiled and waved. He stopped another student going down the stairs toward us.

"Aren't you supposed to be taking the test for Stuyvesant?" Seabrook asked him.

"No," the boy said. "I'm taking the test for Brooklyn Tech. That's next week."

"We get quite a lot of them into the special high schools," Seabrook told me. "More each year. I've made a rule which I try my damnedest to enforce, that each eighth-grader has to take the tests for at least two special high schools."

While Seabrook talked to a teacher in the corridor, I looked in on a science class. All but one of the students were working on various research projects. The exception was at the desk of the bearded black teacher who, tieless, was in his shirt-sleeves. "Liquid state and solid state," the teacher was saying. "Tell me again, José. Tell me the difference. Get it together now, and tell me."

Across the hallway, a tall, solemn teacher was telling two protesting students, "I cannot in conscience give you above a 90 unless you involve yourselves *beyond* homework and exams. You have to participate much more actively in class discussion." The students listened morosely, and started protesting again.

"Hey, Renaldo!" I heard Seabrook's voice in the corridor. The principal had flagged a thin, wiry boy. "I want to talk to you."

"I want to talk to you, Mr. Seabrook," the boy said. "That's not fair, sending for my parents. You know that's what Mr. Hilzen says he's going to do. Jesus, Mr. Seabrook, in all my classes I'm going to get honors."

"You want to bet, Renaldo?" Seabrook said, smiling. "Listen, you made a contract with Mr. Hilzen, and you broke it. The contract says that if you break it, your parents get sent for."

"Aw, Mr. Seabrook, it was my brother that was fighting. It's his problem. I was just standing there."

"That's not what I heard," the principal said. "You come see me later."

"Just standing there." Seabrook shook his head. "He was in

the thick of it. So that breaks the contract." I asked to see the contract they were referring to, and Seabrook got it for me. Renaldo had entered into the agreement two months before. It was on a sheet of lined composition paper:

I, Renaldo Rodriguez, from now on will:

1. Hold my temper
2. Not be a marshal in the lunchroom
3. No fights in school
4. Go to all classes
5. Improve my reading score to 7.9 by June
6. No drinking or coming to school drinking
7. I will not stick with Michael during classes
8. Won't bring a radio to school
9. I will stay on my own floor
10. I will get a conduct card every day from Mr. Hilzen
11. I will not smoke in school

If I break these rules, I understand that my parents will have to come to school.

Below the boy's signature was the signature of a witness— Mr. Hilzen.

"A contract's a contract, right?" Seabrook said. "You break it, you take the consequences. Now, that's a learning experience."

Going through the school, I had noticed that in nearly every classroom there was more than one adult, and I asked Seabrook how I.S. 44 managed to have so much extra help.

"We always have a lot of extra personnel," Seabrook said. "We get student teachers from Hunter, N.Y.U., Fordham, City College, Teachers College. Many of them ask to come here, and many are sent here by their college placement supervisors, who feel they can get good experience here. It works out well for us, too. We've gotten most of our younger teachers and instructors from people who have trained here. One thing we demand of all student teachers is that each of them, in addition to the usual classroom work, give one period a day to tutoring. One student teacher to one kid, or maybe two kids to a student teacher.

"Some of our paraprofessionals," Seabrook added, "also tutor as well as work in the classrooms with teachers. We have more paras, I think, than any other junior high school in this city."

"Are they on a career ladder?" I asked. "Can they go on to become teachers?"

"Oh yes," Seabrook said, "but I don't like the 'ladder' concept. It takes too long and I've seen paras get locked in on that so-called vertical ladder. I'm in favor of career lattices so that people can move more freely—and quickly." We were passing a classroom that was part of the Reading Power Commune. Seabrook pointed to a young black woman working with several children. "There's a paraprofessional," Seabrook said, "who has already been trained here to be a reading diagnostician. Now she's about to go to Fordham on a full scholarship. We have other paras in the same program. They'll all continue to work here, and we'll arrange their schedules so they can do both. They're goddamn good paras, and they're going to be goddamn good teachers. And they *know* Third World kids can learn because they see it happening here every day. This school now has a momentum going. Look at this."

Seabrook handed me a current school report to parents. He pointed to a passage in a section written by A. A. Cherney, assistant principal in charge of supervision: "[During the school year] the Reading Power Commune students, all of them 'Third World' children, outperformed *on an absolute basis the rest of the school. Thus, we see that our Black and Hispanic students can achieve when given the resources and the kind of attention they need.*"

"I'm glad I didn't walk away from I.S. 44," Seabrook said.

"We've proved it again. And as word gets around of what we're doing, of what's happening with Third World kids in other places, we're going to have a lot of Third World parents convinced that their kids *can* learn, and hey, man, we'll be on our way. Because then parents are not going to stand for there being anyone in their children's schools who *doesn't* believe that. You hear me?"

Educating
the Uneducables

Although Luther Seabrook and Martin Schor are of markedly different backgrounds, with few shared interests outside of school, they are very much akin as adults responsible for educating the young. Both hold the teachers in their schools directly accountable when children fail. Both genuinely try to hold themselves accountable when teachers and children fail. Both are acutely conscious of the fact, to quote Kenneth Clark again, that decisions are made in the first grade that can affect youngsters for the rest of their lives. And in the second grade, and in the third, and on to "accepting" one's seemingly irredeemable dumbness or finding out that one isn't dumb after all.

Yet even at a school that reads and at a school that has been turned around, there are always the unreachables, the uneducables, the disruptives, the scourges of even the most industriously understanding teachers and principals. What is to be done with them? For them?

I have known a good many uneducables through the years. One in particular will not leave my mind. Before I started covering schools, I did some reporting on youth gangs and youth workers. One of the gangs was led by a teen-ager I will call Carlos.

One night, the youth worker attached to Carlos's gang and I were involved in an expedition. He and I were in front, closely followed by a half dozen gang members, including Carlos. It was pitch black, the youth worker feeling the way along the walls of a cellar that would lead us to a gym in the basement of a church. We were taking this Stygian route because two of the wildcat warriors in our party had been banned by an elderly priest who had once lived his life secure in his infinite capacity for love of the poor, especially the children of the poor. In recent months, however, the priest was beginning to look as if he were going to end his sour nights in a Graham Greene novel. He was sorely doubting his capacity to love the children of the poor because he had come to know Carlos and some of his friends. Anyway, we were burrowing into his church on the thesis that if the two kids he had kicked out did not come through the front door, the priest would never know they were inside again.

"All Puerto Ricans," the gang members stoutly maintained, "look alike to that mother."

As we slithered through the cellar, a soft voice I knew all too well enlivened the darkness. "Hey," said Carlos to his colleagues behind us, "why don't we waste the reporter and the youth worker?"

There was general laughter, the youth worker's being a bit too hearty, I thought. I cackled softly, to be polite; but knowing Carlos, I was not all that sure I would see another morning. Finally, though, we left the blackness for one of the most cheerful sights I have seen—a sweaty, crummy basketball game in a church basement.

"Carlos could have done it, you know," I said to the youth worker. "A sudden towering urge, a rush of 'Why the hell not?' And we'd have been on page four of the *Daily News*, head down."

"But the thing is," the youth worker said, "he didn't do it. He might have a year ago. In fact, he came very close with that kid he stabbed in the throat. But he's changed. Or at least he's changing."

And so Carlos was. A total, roaring failure in school from as far back as anyone could remember, Carlos had found in this youth worker, and in a couple of others, adults he could talk to, call up in the middle of the night, lean on, learn from. I don't mean to romanticize what was going on. He was still a dangerous kid whom I had not wanted behind me in that black cellar. But dimly, remotely, there might now be some options for him other than a nasty, brutish, and probably short life during which he would nastily shorten others' lives.

Although he had been labeled retarded in an elementary school where no one on the staff spoke Spanish, at a time when Carlos spoke only Spanish, he was bright. Not only street sharp but with a taste for abstract reasoning. This was in the early 1960s, and Carlos, as I discovered in long conversations, was a very knowledgeable fan of the Warren Court's rulings on the rights of defendants. (It took quite a while for this aspect of Carlos to come out. First he and I had talked a lot about boxing, when he learned that I used to be a fight announcer. Then, since we had that in common, Carlos decided I might be worth talking to about other concerns of his.)

Carlos's absorption in such decisions of the Warren Court as the *Miranda* ruling resulted in part, of course, from his keen survival interest in that branch of constitutional law, but it was also due to his genuine fascination with the processes of logic and history which powered such concepts as "due process" and other restraints on the state.

I told him he ought to think about going to law school.

"Shit, man," he said. "I ain't been to high school in a year and a half."

That news, which did not surprise me, was nonetheless depressing. This waste of mind and spirit because his teachers had known Carlos only as an exceedingly dumb and dangerous boy. The latter he certainly was, but no one along Carlos's school odyssey had apparently ever found out how dead wrong the former diagnosis was. Would he have been so dangerous if he had not also been regarded for so long as so dumb, so uneducable?

I don't know what eventually happened to Carlos. The youth workers' program in his neighborhood was shut down. A budget cut. For a few months, I heard stories about him, some of them quite chilling. I suppose it is possible he finally got a steady job and is now a vociferous member of the PTA where his kids go to school, but I do not think so. I think Carlos has been wasted. And who knows how many he has wasted?

Somewhere along the line, I had checked with some of the schools Carlos had so intermittently attended. At each place, I was told pretty much the same thing—by teachers, by principals. "We didn't know what to do with him. We tried, but nothing worked."

I'm sure they tried, some of them anyway, but it may well have been that for Carlos, and a good many youngsters like Carlos, the regular school setting—even if it's a school that reads and has been turned around—is not enough. Is not nearly enough. On the other hand, the youth workers, so long as they were there, had had some effect on Carlos. First, because they had earned his trust. Second, because they continually made clear to him their conviction that he had the potential to be more than a street punk. And third, because they were available when, for whatever reason, he felt he had to speak to an adult he respected. Once, I remember, the imperious code of honor of the streets was operating to force Carlos into a confrontation with another gang leader. Feeling decidedly ambivalent about the necessity for the violence to come, he reached one of the youth workers late one night and after a long session, let himself be talked out of the combat.

As the years went on, I came across a lot of kids whom the

schools did not know what to do with. It was clear that insofar as they came to school, they needed a particular kind of pervasive support which most teachers do not have the skills or patience to provide. Also, they needed more time from those teachers with whom they did connect than most teachers are willing or able to give. Not only time inside school, but time after school, at the point when a crisis was building in their lives—a crisis that had no direct relationship to their schoolwork except that it made it impossible for them to concentrate on their schoolwork.

What kind of education could there be for such kids? I asked this of Luther Seabrook one afternoon at I.S. 44. He didn't have any such kids in his school, I said, but he must have some ideas on the subject.

"What makes you think I don't have any kids like that?" Seabrook said. "I damned well have changed this school, but I haven't make it perfect."

"What do you do with them?"

"Well," Seabrook told me, "there is a guy named John Simon."

John Simon is a New York City teacher in his early thirties who often notes with fierce glee that he has never taken a course in education. (His field was literature, with particular focus on Samuel Beckett.) Simon, moreover, although technically on the staff of Intermediate School 44 on Manhattan's West Side, does not teach in a regular school building, but rather in the large, well-lit, comfortable basement of All Angels Episcopal Church on a dingy block three streets away from I.S. 44. In this decidedly informal setting, Simon, two aids, and several volunteers are stubbornly, unsentimentally, and successfully implementing their conviction that no child is "uneducable"—most certainly not those so categorized by public school systems.

Most of Simon's students, for instance, were sent to him, with great relief, by I.S. 44. Some had been officially labeled "emotionally disturbed," "disruptive," "violent," and "retarded." A few had mugged their fellow students in the very corridors of I.S. 44, others had set fires in the school, and there were those who had seldom attended school at all. Nearly all of these Puerto Rican and black youngsters had been seemingly irredeemable academic failures.

When Hector started coming to the church basement at the age of twelve, a reading specialist at I.S. 44 told John Simon that the boy would never learn to read because he had a "mental block." (The same child had spent most of his elementary school years in classes for children with retarded mental development.)

"It's true," says Simon, a tall, wiry, bearded man, "that when Hector started here, he did not know most of the alphabet, nor did he know the sounds different letters could make. He was able to recognize *cat,* but didn't know how to sound *pat.* For a while, he was climbing and running all over the place, but I kept at him until we connected."

(The teaching in Simon's class is doggedly individualized. As one of the students says, "John and the others, they teach us not like teachers. I mean, man, it's not like those other schools where the teacher goes ahead whether you know what the hell's happening or not. Here you pull on a teacher when you need him. Maybe you get him for an hour. Or, if you want, you can go somewhere by yourself to read.")

"Hector was very impatient," Simon continued the story of the boy who would never be able to read. "He wanted me to just *tell* him the words rather than having to figure them out himself. Finally I said I would, but he had to learn each word he asked for and he had to remember it the next day. So we got a book for second-grade readers, and it took us three days to get through the first page. Hector did not know a single one of those words. He had to learn them all. Each night he took home ten words, put them in a notebook, and the next morning he'd insist I mark a big 100 percent on the page when he had proved he knew what words meant and could read them. Eventually we got through the whole book. It took us two months." On that day of triumph, Hector and John Simon rushed over to I.S. 44 and Hector read the book aloud to Luther Seabrook and to the reading specialist whose prediction Hector was now demolishing.

"This year," Simon points out, "Hector has been reading more difficult books. You see, once he could do a little, he found he could do more, and then more. He's still not an obsessive reader, by any means. He doesn't much like to read to himself. But he keeps discovering he can read parts of newspapers, labels on cans, and other print he comes across, and that pleases him very much."

The degree of patience required of Simon so that Hector could read extends, in different ways for different problems, to each of the twenty-five or so boys, from eleven to nineteen, in the class at All Angels Church. (The junior high youngsters from I.S. 44 are there in the morning, and some stay in the afternoon for more math and reading, or to learn electronics from a volunteer specialist. Around noon, a new student body arrives—graduates of Simon's class who now attend high school but get credit for continued work in the church basement on academics or electronics.)

Simon puts in a long day that often reaches into the evening. He and other members of the staff also spend much of their weekends and summers with the boys. "That means something, you know, the time they put in," Michael, a nineteen-year-old in the program, told me. "We used to mess up in school, right? At I.S. 44, I couldn't read, I couldn't do math, I couldn't do nothing. And the teachers, they didn't even call up my mother. They didn't care about me, so I felt the same way about them, and I messed up some more. But with John, that's a lot harder to do. Every day he stays here until seven, until eight, until whatever problems we got that day are solved. He's got a wife and a baby at home, so why is he doing all this for us? He must care a lot about us, right? Those teachers at I.S. 44, no matter what, they went home at three."

The youngsters now have, as one of them puts it, "a heavy confidence toward ourselves." One reason is the extensive accessibility of the staff. Another is the setting in which they learn.

"When they were in a school with twelve hundred other kids," John Simon emphasizes, "our kids, quite aware they were drowning, could attract attention mainly by doing something outrageous—setting a fire or taking a swing at the school cop. If you asked them why they did these things, they couldn't have told you, except by saying that the school made them angry. Clearly, it made sense to take them somewhere else. A place that continually makes you angry is not a good place to acquire complex academic skills."

When I first went to watch the class in the church basement, it took me a while to realize I was in a classroom. At about half past nine in the morning, as I came down the church stairs, I saw, at the near end of the spacious room, a fourteen-year-old lying on a nondescript couch which might have been beige at a much earlier stage of its existence. He was smoking a cigarette as he read a book. Another youngster came over to the couch, knocked the book out of the first boy's hands, and they started to wrestle.

At a worktable in the center of the room, two boys facing each other were reading—each oblivious to the other and to the more or less mock battle that was taking place on the couch. At a longer worktable toward the far end of the room, near the entrance to the large kitchen where the students and the staff eat together, John Simon was working on reading assignments with three boys. In a corner, Miriam Chalfin, a former New York City schoolteacher and now a full-time volunteer teacher in the basement, was seated next to a boy with whom she was slowly, word by word, going through the first page of a book that was new to the youngster.

During the next half hour, other boys wandered in, sat down to study by themselves, or were joined by one of the teachers in a review of an ongoing assignment. A tall, husky youngster, who came in last of all, appeared to be avoiding John Simon, but the latter, coming up behind him, pushed the boy into a chair.

"Ricardo is dying to do some reading today—he can't wait to start," Simon said to me as he nodded toward the boy, who grimaced and tried to get up from the chair.

"You promised me two pages today," Simon said, pushing him down again. "Hey!" Simon turned around as one student began loudly chasing another in the center of the room. "Stop running around like a couple of little kids." He turned his attention back to Ricardo, but before the reading could start, a lithe black youngster had whizzed by Ricardo, cuffing him on the head.

Simon chased the hit-and-run student, picked him up, and whirled him around in circles. Laughing, the black youngster sputtered, "I'll stop, John, I'll stop."

"I got your word on that, George." Simon stared at him.

The black youngster nodded just as Ricardo, coming up behind him, punched George in the small of the back.

"Damn it, Ricardo," Simon said, "if you keep it up, George will keep it up."

"There is an end to my playing"—George glared at Ricardo —"and the end has come now." As George advanced on Ricardo, Simon grabbed George and applied a hammerlock. "O.K." George was laughing again. "I promise, I really promise."

As Simon sat down next to Ricardo and picked up the book, Ricardo said, "I don't want to read no more, John. I get nervous."

"I'm going to scramble you for breakfast. You haven't read *anything*."

"These words are too hard, man."

"Ricardo, I am going to smack you into next week. There is *nothing* hard on this page. Now, you've got to do the two pages. You can warm up on some easy words. Just keep your eyes on the page instead of playing around."

Fifteen minutes later, Ricardo had finished the two pages. "Was that so painful?" Simon asked.

"Yes," Ricardo said.

I had been looking around the room and mentioned to Simon that the wall colors—red, blue, and lavender—were certainly unlike any I had ever seen in a public school. "The kids painted it all," he said. "Ricardo calls it Puerto Rican funeral parlor décor. But that's what they wanted. This is their room, after all. It's like a clubhouse. You know, every kid likes to have a clubhouse of one kind or another that he can decorate and arrange any way he likes. It gives him a kind of power over the environment that usually only parents and other adults have. And when kids have a place that *is* their own, they respect it and want to spend a lot of time in it. Like here. They decorate it, keep it clean, and see it not only as a classroom but as a place where they can do other things they want to. They'll often stay long after class listening to records, making things, talking, or even sleeping. And in the summer, this same room is our headquarters for various projects. It's a hell of a lot different from the classrooms they've been in before. They don't associate *this* place with anxiety and fear."

Simon went off to a math session with two of the boys, and a small, open-faced, enormously energetic youngster with whom I had been talking earlier in the morning walked over and gave me a notebook of his stories to read.

"If you don't like them, tell me," he said. "I won't be hurt or disappointed."

The boy's style was vivid, the narratives swift and logical, and so I told him.

"Yes, that's good work," said John Simon, who had come over briefly and was reading the last story with me. "But they could even be better, Mikey"—he looked at the boy—"if you cut out a lot of these *ands* and come to a stop every once in a while."

"When I start writing, John," Mikey said, "I get excited. I can't stop."

"This is some writing," Simon said to me, "from a kid who never went to I.S. 44, although he was supposed to be there. He couldn't write anything when he came here. All he knew was how to cut school."

"Oh, he was at 44 once in a while," another boy said. "He was there to beat kids up."

"Yeah." Mikey looked at me. "I used to get mad, all right, and I beat up a lot of people when they started with me. They really got hurt. But then I had to grow up, you know. I can't be doing what I did when I was small. That's why this place is so important to me, you know. If I wouldn't be here, man, I don't know where I would be."

After lunch, I told Miriam Chalfin how impressed I was with Mikey—not only with the strength of his writing, but also with the perceptiveness and candor of his conversation.

"You have no idea," she said, "how good we feel about him. When Mikey first came, he was like a brutalized child. There was almost no core left to him. He'd started with a bad home life. His mother is an epileptic, but that was never explained to him, so he lived with her without knowing why she sometimes behaved as she did. Mikey's father is a very physical man who doesn't do a lot of talking. His way of communicating with Mikey was by hitting him.

"From that home," she continued, "Mikey went to schools that didn't begin to understand how to deal with him. He'd be thrown out of rooms and he'd also be physically abused by some of the teachers. So when we first knew him, Mikey was a wild, intensely scattered, off-the-wall kid, throwing temper tantrums, getting so out of hand that at times he'd have to be held down, literally held down, for half an hour before he'd stop erupting. But now he's got confidence in himself. He doesn't have to blow up." She smiled at Mikey, who had wandered over. "At least he doesn't blow up like he used to."

"That's right," Mikey said. "You know"—he turned to me— "in the hospital, the doctor said I had a good brain. But my mother and father weren't sure. And the teachers in the other school, they didn't bother to look."

"Hey!" Ricardo shouted from the couch as George leaped on him. Ricardo drew back his fist, but John Simon, looking up from a worktable, said, "No, don't do that. Tickle him a little. It's much more effective."

Mikey laughed. "You wouldn't believe it right now," he told me, "but we're all like brothers here. We care about each other. The teachers, too. They're not really teachers—they help us. Like John, he helps my mother a lot with the welfare. And if one of us gets sick, Miriam or John takes us to the medical center. They even take us there for eye examinations, man, if they think there's something wrong."

"John helps us in another way, too," one of the older boys said. "A lot of people, most people, they bullshit you. John levels with you. All the time. And you can't bullshit him either. I don't even bother, because I know he's not going to fall for it."

The first twenty-six years of John Simon's life did not appear to be pointing him toward a career as a teacher of the unteachable. Born in Richmond, Virginia, raised in middle-class comfort in Pleasantville, New York, Simon was graduated from Hamilton College and then spent nine years in intermittent graduate work, six of them in Europe at, among other institutions, the Sorbonne and Cambridge University.

"I studied literature," he says, "an exercise I understand to consist primarily of learning to discriminate among values and value systems. Contrary to what most people seem to feel, I think I had the best possible preparation for my current work."

Back in the United States in 1970, Simon had decided not to write his doctoral thesis on the works of Samuel Beckett. "After all those years in universities," he says, "I felt it was time to see if I could really do something, if I could deal with people rather than just books." Simon did do some work for a publishing firm involved in developing preschool learning materials, and while visiting day care centers, he met Dorothy Pitman Hughes, a formidable organizer of day care centers and people on Manhattan's West Side. Simon became a volunteer worker at the Youth Development Center, part of the West Side Community Alliance, a community service organization which Dorothy Pitman Hughes heads.

"We're an advocacy group for poor people," she notes, "and John, as we came to see, seemed to be a very creative advocate indeed. So I offered him a job as director of our Youth Development Center." In addition to dealing with youngsters, the job got Simon deeply involved in organizing tenants of welfare hotels, fighting attempts to restrict eligibility criteria for day care centers, and orchestrating such demonstrations as the taking over, by poor people, of the city's Human Resources Administration office for seven days.

"I guess you could call this period the dawning of my social and political consciousness," Simon says dryly, "although it had been awakening, to some extent, while I was in Europe. I read two books there I should have read long before—*The Autobiography of Malcolm X* and Eldridge Cleaver's *Soul on Ice.*"

The time spent organizing welfare hotels also awakened Simon to the severe problems of many of the children in those hotels. "We realized," he recalls, "that in our neighborhood there were hundreds of those kids who weren't going to school. They had been beaten around like Ping-pong balls from hotel to hotel, from welfare center to welfare center, all around the city. We started working on a program to help those kids—as well as the welfare children who were in school but were having a really tough time trying to function in a classroom because they had so many other problems outside of school. Then gradually, as welfare hotels were closed down or families were moved out, the schools we were working with started saying, 'We've got this kid, he doesn't live in a welfare hotel, but he has a hell of a problem.' So we established a school intervention project from the elementary through the intermediate grades."

Through federal and city funding, Simon's staff at the Youth Development Center increased from four to thirty-four in a year; and although the project helped some youngsters, it failed many others. Because Simon, as an administrator, had to spend almost all his time on paper work, he had little chance to work directly with the kids in the program. "It was just killing me," he says. "I wanted to be with the kids and find out why they were failing. Hell, I hadn't gone into this kind of work to deal with paper."

Simon resigned as director of the Youth Development Center and tried to figure out a way to set up a smaller, more clearly focused project in which he, and those working with him, would not become submerged in administrative details. One of the schools with which Simon had worked in setting up intervention programs had been Intermediate School 44, and one morning Simon, now unemployed, was talking with that school's astute, blunt, and chronically curious principal, Luther Seabrook. As in the past, Simon was being critical of certain aspects of Seabrook's stewardship of the school.

"This school," Simon told the principal, "is least helpful to the kids who need the most help."

"You know," Seabrook said, "you're always criticizing what I do. O.K., what would *you* do better? I don't have any kind of real job for you, but there's a per diem slot I could probably put you in. What would you do with it?"

Simon proposed taking out of I.S. 44 a number of kids who

were the most trouble to themselves and to the school. He would find another place for them, but for the project to have a chance to work, Simon added, Seabrook would have to agree that staff members of I.S. 44 would not be continually supervising what was going on. "If they're looking over our shoulders all the time," Simon said, "they can kill the whole thing."

Another part of Simon's plan was that each youngster coming into the project would have to enter into a learning contract with Simon and the staff, a contract calling for responsibilities and obligations on each side.

Seabrook thought for a while and then, with a characteristic look of amused respect for anyone willing to festoon himself with hazards, Seabrook said, "O.K., I like the idea of the contract with the kids. But every parent of every kid in that class has to indicate, in writing, that he understands what's going on and that he approves of it. And you can teach the kids any way you want *provided* you produce the kinds of test scores and other academic results that will show me the project is going in the right direction. You can trust me not to supervise the program to the extent of imposing my own ideas on it, but I will have it monitored very carefully to see that it's really working."

By March 1973, space for the class had been arranged in the basement of All Angels Church. There were five youngsters to begin with, and the agreement into which they entered has proved to be the fundamental "social contract" between students and staff ever since. The essential provisions of the contract are:

The adults will not act like cops so long as the students don't force us to by extreme anti-social behavior. On the other hand, if adults get mad, they don't have to hide their anger.

The adults won't squeal on the kids unless they feel absolutely compelled to for the students' own well-being.

Students cannot come in high or get high, bother a student who is working, pick on weaker members of the class, show intentional disrespect, or avoid work entirely.

Students will not be required to do busy work or put in meaningless time. They must, however, take a genuine interest in improving their skills and in learning to cope with the world around them. They must show evidence of this interest through hard and consistent work.

The students must respect the conditions set by the church for our tenancy. In return, we can make our room as comfortable and attractive as our means permit.

Since the class started, only one student has rejected the contract, and he eventually dropped out of school entirely. From time to time, however, there has been a considerable amount of backsliding on the part of some of the youngsters, and when that happens, the staff tries—mightily, as is sometimes necessary—to act on John Simon's dictum that while certain kinds of behavior are to be rejected, the student engaging in that behavior is never to be rejected.

"It is not easy," a teacher told me. "Every once in a while, there are kids I want to knock against the wall, but then I remember how far they've come. For instance, some of them, when they first came here, just did not care about themselves. Like José. He never washed himself, his clothes were raggedy, he looked like a bum in the street. Hell, he went out of his way to *find* clothes that were raggedy. He wanted everybody to say, 'Hey, there goes José. What a mess he is.' And he really was a mess. So we leaned on him, we kept leaning on him, and now he does care about himself. He doesn't look like a bum anymore, and there are days when he'll put three hours of unbelievably sustained concentration into the division of fractions, something he *never* thought he could do before.

"But back on José's block, there are kids his age making a lot of money selling dope. He wants money, too, and while we get the kids jobs, they don't pay all that much. So the pressure's on him. I know some guys are trying to get him to push stuff, and others are after him to mug and steal with them. José keeps saying no. It's hard for José to say no. Meanwhile he's also under another kind of pressure. He knows now he can do good, solid academic work, but he's far from sure he can keep pushing himself in *that* direction and keep living up to *that* standard."

Late one afternoon, José, who had been starting a lot of fights in the class in recent weeks, was the sole item on the agenda of a meeting of the students and the staff. As the agenda, he was present. Several of the youngsters kept pressing José to agree to stop fighting because the fights he instigated took away from the learning time of everybody else. There was no response from José until he was asked directly, "You gonna stop it now? You gonna cut it out?"

"I don't know," José said.

The same question was asked him again and again. His answer remained the same until he finally exploded, "I don't care, damn it! You understand? I don't give a goddamn. I don't care what you're saying!"

Another boy, who himself had hardly acquired a reputation as a pacifist, stepped in front of the accused, and said, "José, you're hurting me when you say that. When you say, 'I don't care,' you're saying the hell with us, the hell with all of us. That's a hurting thing."

José stomped out of the meeting. Later, John Simon caught up with him on the street outside the church. "You've put your whole relationship with the rest of us in jeopardy," he told the boy. "And I *know* you care about this group. I *know* that of all the places you've been, it's the only place you've wanted to stay. And damn it, you know the other teachers and I have taught you more than all the rest of your teachers put together. You don't think of yourself as a stupid person anymore. You can't tell me you don't care about that."

"Yeah," José mumbled. "But listen, John, there's the José you think I am, and there's the real me. And when I get to fighting, that's the real me. I'm tired of trying to be your kind of José, because it's harder to be that. I may like to be it, but it's harder. So I'm never coming back."

"The next morning," John Simon says, "José wasn't here when class started, and he wasn't here at ten or at eleven. But at eleven-thirty, in he came with a suitcase that was filled with everything we had ever given him. We give the kids birthday presents, and all kinds of stuff. José left the suitcase on the floor, and with a little smile, he said, 'Good morning,' and left.

"I kept my eyes away from that suitcase as best I could, because inside was the corpse of two years' work. It just tore me up. A couple of hours later, one of the kids told me he'd seen José on the street, high as a kite. That wouldn't have happened to him if he'd stayed with us. I was worried as hell. What would he do to himself over the weekend? What the hell was I going to do about him?"

Later that afternoon, John Simon's wife, Hannele, a slender, quite joyous young woman from Finland, came by the church with their ten-month-old son, Mikko Jonathan. She was on the way to the supermarket at the corner of the street, and Simon had agreed to watch the baby while his wife shopped. As they started down the street, Simon saw José on the other side, ran across, tackled him, wrestled with him, and when they stopped, tired and laughing, Simon said, "That stuff you brought back this morning—you can't bring it back. I won't accept it. Come on, we got to go to the supermarket."

"Naw," José said, moving away from Simon.

The teacher grabbed him. "I didn't *ask* you to come, I *told* you to come. Now you listen to me. I don't care what you say about which José you are. You are the José I think you are. And maybe you can run away from me now, but I'm gonna come looking for you tomorrow, and you're going to *make it* as the José I think you are because I'm stronger than you. Until you're as strong as I am, and as capable as I am, you're not going to be able to beat me off, and I'm going to come looking for you as often as I have to. Now come on." Simon pulled José along behind Hannele, the carriage, and Mikko inside it.

When they got to the supermarket and Hannele had gone inside, Simon told José, "We are going to stay out here until you get your head in shape, and then, when you're ready to deal with things, we're going back to the class."

After a long talk, José did return to class. "That was a step ahead," Simon told me a couple of weeks later. "There was some more trouble the next week, yet we got a little step ahead out of that one, too. That's the way things go. After all, if I can accept failure from any of our kids, I will get failure. But I do not accept failure."

Working with "educational rejects," John Simon has come to recognize various ways in which kids, no matter how often they have been let down before, can learn how to learn.

"First of all," he says, "you have to listen. When I start working with a kid I don't know too well, I spend a lot of time listening to him before I try to suggest a course of study. I have never fallen in with that dumb notion that you have to start 'teaching' from the very first day of class—as if teaching is something that happens in a vacuum without having to take account of where each student is, in his head, on that first day of class. Where he is and where he's been. So I listen until I have a sense of his particular problems, and then we work together to find out how to resolve them. That way he's already learning. He's analyzing his own problems.

"That kind of preliminary listening by a teacher can reveal all kinds of signals. Take reading. In our class, long before we put a book in a student's hand, we talk with him. We listen to determine the kid's speech patterns, his dialect, and his idio-dialect. We listen for signs of aural confusion, for hints as to how good or how poor the student's ear is. We listen to find out if he knows many or few words, if he can express himself easily or gets frustrated trying to tell a simple story. That way we stay close to the actual source of the student's difficulty. And the other thing, of course, is that any 'curriculum' we develop with a kid is for that kid. And not for another kid. Each is starting in a different place, with different problems."

There is Randall, for instance. At sixteen, new in class, Randall had a reading vocabulary of eight words and had spent most of his school life in classes for the retarded. That is, he had been assigned to those classes, but was seldom present. Each year, once Randall saw that it was not going to happen, that he was not going to learn to read this time either, he abandoned school.

Hearing the depth of the boy's frustration, Simon made a contract with him. Randall need not come to class for more than forty-five minutes a day, but during those forty-five minutes, he had to work hard. Randall agreed, but at first, because he was so embarrassed at not being able to read, he insisted that Simon work with him in private. They studied in a stairwell of the church. Within four months, Randall was out of the stairwell and reading in class.

"If I had paid any attention to Randall's records, his IQ, or his reputation," Simon told me, "I probably would have gotten discouraged before he had had a chance not to be discouraged. But because we both believed Randall could read, he learned to, and every official school prediction about him has been completely turned around."

Another boy, Herman, was convinced he was stupid. His family believes that one reason he held to that despairing self-diagnosis so long has to do with the fact that he knew no English when he first entered the New York City school system. During Herman's first two years in that system, his teacher, knowing no Spanish, put Herman's desk in a corner, gave him crayons to keep him busy, and ignored him entirely. In any case, by the time he was in the fifth grade in another school, Herman suddenly decided that, dumb or not, he wanted to learn to read. He began taking books home and reading them over the weekend, but by the end of that school year, he had scored only a 2.9 on the city-wide reading tests.

That fall, Herman became part of John Simon's class and after several months of work with one of the teachers, Herman had scored a 6.0 on the same city-wide test. As Simon observes, "If that test has any validity, it is all but impossible for anyone to improve that much in so short a time. It *is* possible, however, for someone with the necessary skills—which Herman had been acquiring on his own—to gain enough poise and confidence to improve his score that much if the earlier score reflects poor attitude more accurately than low ability.

"Listening to Herman," Simon continues, "we had recognized that *his* problem was low self-esteem. So the teacher who worked with him here was valuable not so much in teaching Herman how to decode written language, but in convincing him to stop making excuses for himself, stop playing around, and get on with the job of teaching himself how to read. Once Herman had gained enough confidence to make that decision, all we had to do was limit his distractions and be available when he genuinely needed us. Herman did the rest by himself."

In the terminology of courses in education, John Simon's concern as a teacher is with "the whole child," each child being challengingly and sometimes maddeningly distinctive. But in terms of what goes on in his classroom, Simon's way of enabling "the whole child" to function in a school is not to be found in most education texts.

"Any adult remembers how plain physically uncomfortable school can be," Simon says. "You can't eat when you're hungry; you can't get up and walk around when you feel cramped; you can't shout when you're angry; and you can never, never be alone. Well, we avoid a lot of problems that come from that kind of constriction by never creating them. The kids can eat, curse, play, shoot craps, or sleep. They cannot, as the contract says, come in high or get high, bully anyone, bug a student who's working, or not do any work themselves. But once they've done their work, they're not forced to stay in the classroom just because this is school. After an hour of difficult reading, for instance, a kid's better off taking a break in the fresh air if that's what he feels like doing. Because if he doesn't get that break, he could well wind up bothering the rest of the class. And sometimes, when a kid is indeed bothering the rest of the class by picking fights, I or someone else on the staff will take him out on the street and we'll go for a walk to try to find out why he's fighting so much.

"It's our job, it's any teacher's job," Simon continues, "to know a kid as well as we can. I mean, we struggle to help our students learn to read and write and get all the other essential skills, but we also try not to forget that they were people before they came to the school and will still be people when they leave. They have bodily functions, quite sensitive personal problems, and all the rest of the baggage all of us carry around from cradle to grave. In this school, our kids know they can come to us with anything that's bothering them, including things like sexual problems that they'd be too embarrassed to talk about with anyone else. They also know that if something in their lives becomes overwhelmingly troubling, they can talk about it here, no matter what else is going on. If a kid has just broken up with his girl or has had a big fight with his mother, he knows he's entitled to get it all out here. He knows he's entitled to some special support from the rest of us."

Not only do the students get support, but their parents receive encouragement about their children from Simon and the other members of the staff. There are regular visits to the parents' homes.

"If any of us gets into trouble," Tito, an older student, and one much respected by the other youngsters, told me one morning, "John or another teacher will come to the house, not like a teacher but like a friend, and we'll all talk about it. But they also come when there's no trouble. I never heard of a teacher before who comes to your house and says to your mother, 'Hey, your kid is a fine kid, it's really a lot of fun working with him.' "

John Simon, listening to our conversation, laughed. "Well, for a kid who's always brought home report cards that look like descriptions from the Wanted posters in the post office, some positive reinforcement can go a long way. When a parent tells you that we're the first teachers who ever cared that much about their children to visit their homes, you figure the kid will get stronger support in the home from then on. Furthermore, as we get to absorb the feeling of the home and the quality of the family relationship, obviously we learn more about the kid."

One difficulty with home visits, Simon went on to say, is that since many of the students do not have particularly good relationships with their parents—in part because of the kids' past records in and out of school—the staff people feel they have to be careful as to what the parents are told. "We can't maintain the confidence of our kids," Simon says, "if they're afraid we'll tell their parents too much."

"Does that mean," I asked, "that you seldom tell the parent anything negative about a kid?"

"No," another staff member said. "It depends on how important it is, how important it is to the kid's survival. A few weeks ago, I went to a kid's house to tell his mother he had not been coming to school. Then we *both* yelled at the kid."

"You have to gauge the individual situation," Simon said. "I've gotten to know most of the parents well enough to be able to judge when telling them something negative about their kid will make matters worse rather than better. For example, if a kid smokes a joint once in a while and if the parent is going to beat him up if he knows that, then it makes more sense for us to deal with that in the class, and that's what we do. On the other hand, two years ago a kid got me so mad that even though I'd been told that if his parents heard of anything bad he'd done they'd really beat him up, I went to his home and told them exactly what the kid had done. At that point I didn't care if his father was going to beat the hell out of him. I wanted the message to get through."

The offense took place when Simon and a volunteer teacher of printing had taken the youngster to a printing shop in Queens to help pick up some teaching materials. "Do not touch anything—anything," Simon had told the boy as they went into the shop. Inside, however, while the adults were otherwise occupied, the boy had jammed a Teletype machine.

Simon was still angry about the incident two years later. "It cost the owner about two hundred dollars to fix that machine, and the kid lied about it to him besides, saying he hadn't done it. Here we were in the real world with a guy who was kind enough to give us stuff, and this kid had acted not as part of a group with certain responsibilities, but as a loner, a destructive loner. The kids all have to learn there are things you can do, and there are things you can't do."

A few days after Simon had told me about the incident in the printing shop, another member of the class, in a seizure of anger, had rammed his fist through a window at All Angels Church. I asked one of the staff members what had so enraged the boy.

"That's what we're trying to figure out," the teacher said. "Something's bothering the hell out of him, but he won't tell John or me or anybody. When he gets like that, it's almost impossible to get through to him. John thinks we've got to rattle him, so he's called a meeting."

At the meeting the boy tried to remain expressionless, but he clearly was hurt and embarrassed as John Simon forcefully reminded him of everyone's agreement to abide by the church's conditions for the class's tenancy. One implicit condition was that the church be left intact.

"Listen," Simon said to the boy at the end of the meeting. "We have tried every way we can to understand what's making you do things like this. At this point we care less about whether you have friendly feelings toward us than we care about your *life*. If we have to embarrass you to get that message across and if you're going to resent us for it, then that's what has to happen."

The boy said nothing and walked out of the church.

The next time I came to the class, three days later, the boy was immersed in a reading lesson.

"He finally came to me and told me what his problem is," a staff member told me. "It was later that night, after the meeting."

"What is it?" I asked.

"Oh, he made me promise I wouldn't tell anybody. Not even John."

One night, at the Only Child, a restaurant-bar near All Angels Church, John Simon and several members of his staff were reflecting on education over pitchers of beer and the pungent sounds of a jukebox specializing in jazz and Latin music. An assistant teacher, Chris Sugarman, who is white, seventeen, and on the way to college (but only part-time so that he can stay with the class), was telling of his recent initiation into responsibility by the kids in the class. Sugarman, as I had observed, is an unusually effective tutor in basic skills, but I had wondered about his frequent horsing around with the youngsters. In fact, I had first thought he was one of the students.

"The kids called a meeting a few nights ago," Sugarman was saying. "I had been trying to come down to them, to be like them, and that was really bugging them. They told me they wanted me to set an example and instead I was playing with them, snapping with them—you know, joking—too much."

"They really did land on you," John Simon said.

"Oh, I wasn't upset." Sugarman poured some beer.

"The hell you weren't." Simon laughed. "That's why I had to make a point of taking you aside afterward so I could be sure you realized how much the kids care about you. If they didn't, they wouldn't have bothered having that meeting. They would have just told you to go to hell."

"O.K., I was upset," Sugarman said, smiling. "But I'm glad it happened. They taught me I had to grow up, that I really do have to be an example."

"Being an example is only part of it," said Arthur Powell, who is black, in his early twenties, a student at Hampshire College, and has been an associate of Simon's for the past seven years. He is math program developer for the class. "There's another kind of responsibility I've learned from working with these kids," Powell emphasized. "I once thought the thing for me to do was to offer the kids an ideological system—to educate them politically. But now I know that what they need more than anything else is skills. So I've changed my major from education to math. It's important for them to know math, and kids like these don't really get taught math in the school system."

"Yeah," said Simon, "math and the sciences are like a white preserve. I remember that when we started the class, all the emphasis was on reading, and you're the one who kept forcing the issue so that math was finally included as being of equal importance."

"It's gotten to where I go to the library at Hampshire," Arthur Powell said, "and instead of studying for an exam, I go looking through the card catalogue to find out more things I can do with, say, polyhedrons in teaching the kids. There are easier careers than math for me to follow, but this seems the best way for me to provide the kids what they need."

"You mentioned an ideological system," John Simon broke in. "It's like some of the people who were in the antiwar movement and all the other movements in the 1960s. They felt that you got someplace by being ideologically correct and by having the best of intentions. The fact is—and the kids have taught me this—the difference between what you believe and what you accomplish depends on how much of your beliefs you're able to translate into daily struggle. In our case, we struggle as a small group against the tide. It hasn't been easy, but it also hasn't been futile. And it certainly has been real. And you know, while it's quite possible to leave a movement, it's not possible to leave a group of kids. Not for any of us."

"The kids don't seem to want to leave either," I said. "José and Mikey and some of the others have mentioned the possibility of enlarging the class into a school in which the kids who graduated could come back and be teachers."

"Yes, we've all talked about that," Simon said. "Can you imagine the creative energy these kids, who have seen what can happen in a class, would bring as teachers? Some will come back that way, but I don't see our enlarging the class much beyond what it is. However, what I'd like us to do is take over what they call in New York City a '600 school'—one of those dumping grounds for so-called 'uneducable' kids. We'd throw out all the teachers, lock the doors, sit down with the kids, and say, 'Look, do you think we can do something together? If you do, help us defend this damn place until we've straightened out the takeover with the authorities.'"

There was laughter until I asked whether the class at All Angels Church is, as the foundations ask, replicable. "Can it happen in other neighborhoods, in other cities?"

"The mix is not so special," Simon answered. "I can't think of a place where the pieces couldn't be put together—a community organization, a church, a cooperative public school principal. The question is can you get enough people who think a lot of themselves to believe it's important to spend their time working with a limited number of kids who, at the outset, don't think much of themselves or their teachers or society.

"There should be many people around the country who might be right for this, people who don't want to be cogs in somebody else's machine and are looking for something worth doing. But the tricky part about something like this is that it doesn't come prepackaged. The situation has to be created, and there's no place to learn how to do that. You have to learn that by yourself."

From the start of the class, John Simon and the staff have persistently tried to get after-school jobs for as many of the youngsters as have wanted to work. Some of the jobs have been in day care and youth centers in the neighborhood. "At first," Simon recalls, "our teen-agers, considering themselves tough, balked at working with young kids, but they came to enjoy it. Actually, that kind of work makes a lot of sense for teen-agers like ours. Having to look out for kids less independent than they are, they learn a greater sense of responsibility. They also learn how to work with other people, and since they're in places where they have to use cognitive development materials as part of their job with the little kids, they keep sharpening their own skills."

Other kinds of jobs, paid and unpaid, have developed from the youngsters' pride in Leap-Frog, 120 acres of woods, fields, and a lake in the Catskills. The property was purchased by the class in conjunction with the West Side Community Alliance, and the students have worked in various ways to help raise funds for mortgage payments, maintenance costs, and for an ambitious class project at Leap-Frog—a thirty-foot-diameter plywood geodesic dome, which first required their learning geodesic math and took more than a year to complete.

"For most of our lives, you know," José told me, "we never finished anything we started—a book, homework, you name it. And we didn't believe we'd ever finish the dome. But we did. All by ourselves. Whatever happens, at least we got the dome to be proud of."

So intent were the youngsters on getting the money to finish the dome that they became expert cutters and sellers of fire-wood in Chappaqua, where John Simon's family lives, and net-ted a thousand dollars in profits over eighteen months of chopping. "By reputation," Simon told me, "these are kids who supposedly can't be depended on to be responsible workers. No sticking power. Well, you should have seen them. They cut and split six and seven cords of wood in a day, and it was all very efficiently organized. *They* did the organizing. There's no ques-tion these guys have learned how to work, and they've made more money since doing all kinds of outdoor jobs in Westches-ter County."

Darrill, who had been one of the most diligent fund raisers for the dome project, was experiencing what might be called a relapse during one of the times I came to the class. He had fallen behind in his work, had gotten into more fights than usual, and at one point had smashed a window in the church.

"Why is it always the same window?" John Simon asked no one in particular the day it happened.

"Who pays for it?" I asked.

"I do. That's my Christmas present to everybody," Simon said dourly. "Four goddamn windows already this year!"

Eventually, after several long sessions with an assistant teacher and with Tito, the oldest boy in the class, Darrill more or less simmered down.

"You didn't work with him yourself?" I asked Simon.

"No. In this case, Darrill had a better relationship going with those two. What counts is who can get through. Tito isn't the only student who gets involved in helping to deal with other kids' problems. We don't have that kind of hierarchy here.

Anyway, I know Darrill's problem—success. Before all that happened—the goofing off and the fighting—he had had five very good weeks. He couldn't stand the pressure of having been good that long. That's a hard problem for us to deal with. Think about it. You mug somebody, you get instant gratification or instant turnoff. You've either got money for drugs or you get arrested. A good high or a bad trip. But what's the satisfaction in being good? I mean material satisfaction. Being good only has a long-term payoff. Right now, there's nothing for these kids in being good except the smiles on our faces. That's why we've got to get them better jobs, jobs that pay more than the ones we've been able to work out so far."

One attempt in that direction has been the opening by the class of a city-wide gallery of student craftwork, the Student Design Center, in a small store—a former Chinese laundry— on the same block as All Angels Church. (Everybody in the class pitched in—rewiring the store, installing the burglar alarm, setting up shelves and display cases, putting in the wall-to-wall carpeting, and painting the place yellow, white, and orange.)

The Student Design Center is open to student creators throughout New York City, from day care through college age, from private as well as public schools. Each student sets the price of his work and keeps 65 percent of the sale price. The center gets the rest for expenses, including the salaries of the youngsters in the class who operate the store—from keeping the books to handling publicity.

On the morning of the Student Design Center's grand opening in January 1975, four of the kids were painting several display racks on the sidewalk in front of the store.

"You got a lot more to do?" I asked.

"Not much," one of them said, looking up. "But man, this was some job. Day and night. When we started, that place looked like a junkyard."

At the door, the center's manager, Tito, was greeting neigh-

borhood people, dignitaries, and kids from other parts of the
city, with egalitarian graciousness. Among those already inside
were Luther Seabrook, principal of I.S. 44; Dorothy Pitman
Hughes, head of the West Side Community Alliance; and New
York City Consumer Affairs Commissioner Elinor Guggenheimer. All over the walls and on the shelves was the diversely
attractive, and often quite ingenious, work submitted by students ranging in age from eleven to twenty-two. There were
ponchos, crotcheted vests, shoulder bags, candles, leatherwork,
sculpture, shawls, ash trays, flowerpots, pillows, ink drawings,
and needlepoint.

"You see," Tito was saying to a fourteen-year-old from a
private school who was thinking of offering some of his work
for sale, "we get your phone number, and when we sell your
things, we call you up so you know it's time to get paid and so
you can send us more stuff." The youngster said he'd be back.
"And tell your friends," Tito called after him.

In the center of the store, Commissioner Guggenheimer was
making an offer to John Simon. "We need to fix up our offices
downtown," she said, "so why don't I commission the kids to
decorate one of the rooms, and when it's done, we'll also have
a press conference down there for the Design Center?"

"They'll be big, splashy paintings," Simon told her.

"Oh that'll be lovely," she said. "So cheerful."

"What we should have done," one Puerto Rican boy was
saying to another, "is call the TV stations and tell them a
Puerto Rican terrorist group said they was going to blow up the
store. Then we would have gotten some real coverage, man,
television cameras and all that."

"As hard as it is to stomach," Miriam Chalfin, the full-time
volunteer teacher, was telling me as we leaned against a wall
near the door, "not every one of these kids is going to make it
academically. But my God, how they've developed as people."

"You only expect a few to go to college?" I asked.

"No." John Simon had walked over. "I think it'll be more than a few. Let me answer your question this way. Earlier this year, my father died, and a lot of people who loved and respected him wanted to set up a fund in his name. Our family has put the money into a scholarship fund in trust for those of the kids who will go on to college. I wouldn't have put money given in my father's name into something I didn't think was very realistic. So I do expect many of them to go to college." Since the fund was established, a number of the youngsters have indeed entered colleges which themselves have provided more substantial scholarship grants.

A thin, intense boy darted into the store carrying another display rack. He set it down carefully, waved to Miriam Chalfin, and then worked on rearranging the rack until it suited his sense of perspective.

"I've been working with that one for three years," the teacher said softly, "from before John set up the class. I've poured my life's blood into that child. This was a kid who couldn't put three words together. And wild—was he wild! But now he can express ideas articulately and logically. He writes some marvelous things. But he still has bad times, he gets very depressed."

"Why?" I asked.

"Because he's sixteen years old and he's not sure where he's going. And because he needs money. It's as basic as that. Last week we were working on some math on the couch in the classroom, and he was just too disconsolate to concentrate. I asked him what was bothering him. 'I'm disgusted,' he said. 'I can't stand living at home, I don't have the money to move out, I can't get a job that pays anything, I'm sick of school. That's what's the matter. There's nothing in this world for me.'

" 'O.K.,' I said, and got the classified ads," Miriam Chalfin continued, "and we sat there, going down the page. 'How about typing?' 'I can't type, damn it.' It was the same thing with what few other possibilities there were. So I moralized at him again about the need to stay in school and learn some skills. He didn't say anything, I left for a few minutes, and when I came back, he was lying on the couch, banging his fists into it, and as he looked up and saw me, he said, in *such* anger and frustration, 'I can't even mug anybody anymore, and it's all your fault.'"

"They Don't Give a Damn About Our Kids, Do They?"

Had it not been for John Simon and his equally stubborn and resilient colleagues, most, if not all, of the youngsters going to public school at All Angels Episcopal Church would eventually have become dropouts, thereby joining a good many other dead souls.

On the average, nationally, three out of every four public school students stay the course and get a high school degree. In the big cities, whose public school populations increasingly consist of children of the poor, the percentage of the educationally disenfranchised (because the schools did not know what to do with them) is much higher. Michael Rebell, writing in the winter 1975 *New York University Education Quarterly,* points out, for example, that "Only 51.1 percent of New York City's black students and 44.8 percent of its Hispanic students who entered the ninth grade in 1967 were still enrolled four years later, as compared with 76.1 percent of 'other' students."

The school system has obviously not done well by those "other" youngsters, having failed to educate 23.9 percent of them. But the system's record with regard to black and Hispanic kids is all the more egregiously destructive. Furthermore, Rebell adds that more recent studies indicate the percentage of school dropouts in the city has continued to rise in all categories. Worth keeping in mind, too, are those many youngsters who do somehow stay the route and get a piece of paper rewarding their inertia, but who *also* have not been educated by the public school systems in New York and elsewhere in the country.

One of the latter speaks in Elliot Liebow's book, *Tally's Corner:* " 'I graduated from high school [Baltimore] but I don't know anything. I'm dumb. Most of the time I don't even say I graduated, 'cause then somebody asks me a question and I can't answer it, and they think I was lying about graduating. . . . They graduated me but I don't know anything. I had lousy grades but I guess they wanted to get rid of me.' "

What becomes of them—the dropouts, the pushouts, those who graduate with a "general" diploma but cannot read at more than an eighth-grade level, if that? Well, they don't become "innovative" academics who "prove" the relative unimportance of schooling (e.g., Christopher Jencks, *Inequality: A Reassessment of the Effect of Family and Schooling in America,* 1972). Nor do they become "radical" professors of economics who maintain that until we change our economic system to egalitarian socialism, there's not much that can be fundamentally done to change the schools (e.g., Samuel Bowles and Herbert Gintis, *Schooling in Capitalist America,* 1976).

Instead, these waste products of the public school system slip in and out of low-level jobs or fall off the employment edge entirely into welfare or crime. Or as former secretary of labor Willard Wirtz says mildly, "If a high school diploma is no longer a significant job credential—and it isn't—and if a surprising number of high school age youth aren't even in school, it hardly seems to be ground for optimism that half of all high school graduates now go on to college."

Indeed, the performance of the public schools does not present ground for optimism. And it is of no comfort whatever to read revisionist historians of education who demonstrate that the public schools have always performed poorly with regard to sizable numbers of their poorer charges. History is not necessarily prophecy. If such schools as those in this book have learned how to prevent youngsters—even among the most likely candidates—from dropping out of their potential, then there is no reason to absolve the others. No matter what history shows. Furthermore, as the potential of so many youngsters continues to be ignored or twisted by public schooling, it is, or should be, the shame of the nation that such destruction is allowed to continue.

Now, that's an almost embarrassingly old-fashioned muckraker's phrase—"the shame of the nation." But is it inaccurate? George Weber, the careful, even conservative, assessor of American schooling for the Council for Basic Education, pointed out in the September 1975 bulletin of that organization:

> As the reports of the National Assessment of Educational Progress have shown, the blunt truth is that our schools are failing miserably, scandalously, outrageously, at least 20 per cent of our young people. About this portion leaves our schools after ten to twelve years unable to read in any meaningful sense, unable to write beyond a primitive, inaccurate, and sometimes incoherent level, and unable to compute almost anything at all. Some of these young people, believe it or not, have high school diplomas in their hands.

Yet in what presidential, congressional, state, or municipal campaign in memory has that "scandalously" stunted 20 percent been an important political issue? Oh, perhaps on occasion a candidate from a minority neighborhood may futilely raise the issue, but most politicians have given no serious thought to those defrauded consumers of public schooling. After all, they're getting it free, aren't they?

George Weber goes on to estimate that of the remaining 80

percent of those in elementary and secondary schools, about 5 percent are doing "really outstanding work." And "the great middle group—70 to 75 percent—receive a poor to excellent education depending on which school and which school district they attend."

Nor are only "disadvantaged" kids getting a skimpy education. "There are students," Weber adds, "with very favorable backgrounds who do not achieve what they could. Their education is clearly deficient." And in fact, there are many such students—afflicted, *despite* their family backgrounds, with learning poverty.

Remember again that only about half of all high school graduates go on to college, and of those who do, increasingly sizable numbers need remedial work in basic skills during their first college year, and sometimes beyond. And these are largely white, middle-class kids.

But it is that very low 20 percent which most concerns George Weber: "They achieve so little that it is a disgrace. A disproportionate number of them are 'disadvantaged,' of course, *but what possible excuse can the schools make for giving them nothing or virtually nothing in ten or twelve years?* It is this group, we submit, that the schools should concentrate on in the immediate future." (Emphasis added.)

George Weber's prescription is a logical imperative—if we really do recognize schooling as a quintessential national priority. But actually, schooling is not nearly so intense a national concern. Even when the economy is not in decline, funds are normally insufficient—especially for the 20 percent of the young who, as Weber emphasizes, are "scandalously, outrageously" let down by the schools. Funds to allow for the widespread adoption of the low student-teacher ratio, for example, in John Simon's class for "the uneducables." Funds to hire enough diverse specialists to deal with learning difficulties, including those that have been school-induced (the latter being an educationally iatrogenic condition not limited to the children of the poor). Funds for authentic bilingual education wherever needed. Funds to provide one-to-one instruction in any subject, whenever that intensity of instruction is needed, for a time, to convince a child he is not dumb.

This is not to say that money has not often been wasted by certain schools and districts. And obviously, the presence of additional money cannot guarantee the presence of resourceful principals and teachers with high expectations of themselves and their students. Nonetheless—as this chapter specifically indicates—money does make a difference, frequently a crucial difference.

Take class size, for instance. Most teachers would say, correctly, that an elementary school class should not have more than twenty-two children. Most such classes, however, are considerably larger. And the vast majority of junior high school teachers have to deal with 150 to 200 children a day. "We're supposed to give them individual attention, know their home situations, and counsel them," one teacher says. "But this way I hardly even know their names. We're all drowning in sheer numbers of students. So what's the alternative if you can't get smaller classes? You lower your goals, and that's what many of us have done."

I very clearly remember, for example, several days spent as a visiting lecturer at the Groton School in Massachusetts a few years ago. The average class size ranged from eight to ten, and in not a few classes there were no more than six youngsters. It was a stunning, if obvious, lesson in the effect of economic privilege on education. There is not a school in the country, however slipshod, in which most kids would not learn a great deal more with that degree of individual attention. Even with teachers who would never be hired by Groton.

However, back in our democratic public school systems, while not expecting Groton-style expenditures on education, I have seen, in years of writing about schools, damagingly insufficient funding in "good times," especially, of course, in poor neighborhoods. And in "recessions," the truly low priority of public schooling becomes most instructively evident in practically all neighborhoods.

Consider the economic malaise of the mid-1970s—and such a time, in our chronically unstable economy, is quite likely to come again. The schools were still cripplingly inadequate for the children of the poor, and there were clear indications that more and more children of the middle class were also being harmed. As Gene Maeroff reported in a front-page *New York Times* story in March 1976: "Rising dissatisfaction with the results being achieved by the country's public schools is giving impetus to a movement toward denying youngsters their high school diplomas until they can demonstrate minimum competency in the basic skills."

With these, and a good many other fundamental schooling problems, one might have logically expected a corollary national movement, at least among parents, demanding that schools not be weakened financially at a time when they were obviously in need of remedial regeneration. In fact, however, it was during the mid-1970s that school budgets were being cut so severely in many cities as to provide particularly striking proof of how limited public concern about the public schools actually is.

In Los Angeles (according to the weekly education newspaper, *Education U.S.A.*), School Superintendent William J. Johnston observed in the fall of 1975, "We begin once again the job of dismantling major portions of our educational program ... which is already minimal in many respects." In Oregon, school programs were decimated in the mid-1970s and there were similar massive assaults on education budgets in Illinois, New Jersey, Maryland, Ohio, and a growing number of other states and cities.

In New York City, in the fall of 1975, an official of the Board of Education noted resignedly that the city was headed for "bread and water school programs" for a long time ahead. And so it was.

What follows—the story of a single New York school falling into a state of acute malnutrition—is the story, in essence, of many schools in many parts of the country. It is the kind of story that has taken place in previous economic crunches and that will happen again—unless there finally does emerge a durably organized constituency for the nation's schools that will be able to prevent the gutting of education in times of economic downturn and that will ensure the strengthening of learning in more or less good times.

I also include this chapter to demonstrate the specific effects on a particular faculty and student body of an attitude toward public education by public officials, in New York and elsewhere. To these officials, as one New York City community school board member put it, "education is not even a tertiary concern." The statistics of the bludgeoning budget cuts that come from this attitude, which is not uncommon, are not likely to stay in your mind. Perhaps, however, some of the people in this chapter will.

Furthermore, this is a story of a school that was learning how to enable all kinds of youngsters to learn but was forced to slide back, and is still sliding. Consider this school, too, in the context of predictions by research specialists in urban affairs that in certain large cities, in the decades ahead, school budgets are likely to diminish while, as Thomas Muller of the Urban Institute in Washington, D.C., puts it, "increases in the size of police departments can be expected to continue in response to higher crime incidence."

This makes sense?

A New York City teacher I've known for years to be uncannily resourceful, an expert in both traditional and open classroom techniques, a fierce believer that *all* children can learn, was near tears.

"Have you any idea what these budget cuts have really meant?" she said as she cornered me in the fall of 1975. "I have thirty-eight kids in my class. Some need an awful lot of individual attention, which I can't give them. And the others also need more time than I can possibly give. We have fewer materials than I used to have when I taught in South America in the Peace Corps. And there'll be *more* cuts in the next few months, and then more after that. A million kids in this city are being ripped off. Doesn't anybody care?"

The teacher works in Brooklyn, and I have heard similar explosions of frustration in recent years from teachers in other boroughs. "Don't ever tell me again," one of them said, "that we put a high priority on kids in this country. Did you hear about the principal in Inwood who resigned before Christmas because of the cuts? Everybody always had great respect for him—the kids, the parents, his staff, even the other principals in the district. But he said he would no longer participate in a fraud that was called education. I wish I had his guts."

But the mayor said, and the governor said, that we all had to retrench. Yet while funds for other city agencies were cut by 8 to 11 percent, the school budget was slashed by up to 22 percent. Or as city school chancellor Irving Anker, normally the mildest-mannered of civil servants, has charged: "No other public agency has been as brutalized as education has been in this city."

If this is so, why do we allow it to be so? "Because," a teacher at P.S. 98 (the Shorackappock Elementary School), at the upper end of Manhattan, says bitterly, "kids are invisible. You cut the cops or firemen or garbage collectors, and people get upset. That's an immediate danger. That gets you in the throat. But kids are shut away in those buildings all day long and who knows or cares if they end up stuffing fifty of them into one class? And who sees the damage done to them? It won't show for maybe twenty years. I'm so mad I could spit bullets because *I* see what's happening to those kids every day."

Just as angry is that teacher's principal, Mark Shapiro, who, as the cuts go on, addresses a blistering broadside to Mayor Abraham Beame, with copies sent to city and national education officials, to diverse members of the press, and, for good, futile measure, to the President of the United States.

Accusing the mayor of "dooming countless thousands of children to impoverished adulthood because they had impoverished education as children," Mark Shapiro noted that his elementary school staff has been so crippled by cuts that although substantial progress had been made during the previous three years, the school is now in danger of becoming no more than a custodial institution. With a large number of poor children (although at least a quarter of the parent body is middle class), P.S. 98 still gets federal Title I funds for compensatory education. But, Shapiro thundered, the school has lost 25 percent of its New York City tax-levy teaching positions, half of its guidance counselors and school guards, and more than 40 percent of its paraprofessional assistant teachers.

The kids are unhappy, Shapiro adds, because they have been shifted from teacher to teacher; and the teachers are greatly disturbed because they have to cope with larger classes while under the additional pressure of worrying whether they'll be fired, too, in the next wave of cuts. "Who killed Shorackappock?" the principal angrily asked the mayor.

The principal of Shorackappock (an Indian name for "in the woods," or Inwood) received no response to his indictment or to his demand that the school be restored to educational solvency. ("A restoration of half our cutbacks," Shapiro had emphasized in his letter, "would bring us into line with cutbacks other city agencies have suffered and permit us to offer some sort of viable program.")

Having received a copy of the scorching Shapiro manifesto, I decided to look into conditions at the school because the shaky state of Shorackappock is relatively representative of the impact of the budget cuts on schools in all the boroughs of New York City, and in many other school districts throughout the country. There are schools in worse shape and there are schools in more "advantaged" neighborhoods that are surviving with less trauma. But by and large, this Inwood elementary school reveals much of what happens to public school education whenever the economy falters.

Mark Shapiro, in his early forties, himself a product of the Brooklyn public school system, had been a teacher in Bedford-Stuyvesant, a guidance counselor, and an assistant principal before being approved by a parents' screening committee as principal of Shorackappock in 1971. He accepted the position, Shapiro recalled in the open letter to Mayor Beame, "with great relish, not the least reason being that this is one of the very few truly multi-ethnic schools in New York City and I looked forward to working within what I considered a microcosm of New York City." (Actually, with an 8 percent increase, during 1975, of Spanish-speaking children, the twelve hundred kids in the school at the time of the pronunciamento to the mayor were 60 percent Hispanic, 25 percent white, 12 percent black, and 3 percent Oriental. Still, Shorackappock remains more "multi-ethnic" than most.)

During his tenure, Shapiro has accomplished what a number of educational reformers only suggest in books. He has given the parents a real choice of educational options. There is a standard ("traditional") subschool; an open classroom subschool; and a bilingual subschool, which became so successful that Shorackappock was designated a "Bilingual Pilot School" by the Board of Education. As word spread of the justifiedly high morale among both kids and faculty, parents in the neighborhood who (often at severe financial sacrifice) had placed their children in private and parochial schools began to return them to the public rolls. Until 1975. From September on, as the budget cuts became more and more palpable, the movement back to private and parochial schools began.

But Shorackappock keeps on keeping on. One morning, looking for the principal, whom I knew only by his fiery writing style, I saw that the door to his office was open—as it nearly always is, I later found out—and walked in. In the large, brightly lit room, there were a small desk; boldly colored posters in English and Spanish; and in a glass case, an unusually intriguing relief map of the nation—a project of one of last year's fifth-grade classes. The unidentifiable, seemingly prehistoric material out of which the map had been made was cryptically referred to in a legend at the bottom: "For every 1,000 feet, there is one inch of goop."

A medium-size, wiry man in a leather jacket, blue jeans, and a red-and-white-striped turtleneck came in the door. He was bearded, with a full head of graying black hair. It took me a moment or two to realize he was the principal.

"That map is quite a piece of work, isn't it?" Mark Shapiro said. "The teacher of that class, one of the best fifth-grade classes I've ever seen, was one of our budget casualties."

The principal sat down, returned a wave from two children passing in the hall, and handed me several recent issues of the mimeographed weekly school newsletter, *Shorackappock Scoop.* In one of them, Shapiro had informed the parents that "as part of the citywide cutbacks, the services offered by the school dental clinic have been cut in half, from four days a week to two days a week." The following week's issue included the news that "we have lost the services of our Speech Teacher.... Obviously cutbacks continue. It continues to be most urgent that you voice your concerns to your elected representatives. I urge you again to write in whatever language you feel most comfortable."

"The cuts get worse and worse," Shapiro said to me. "Last year we had a school psychologist two days a week. This year we have none. Zero. I think we're also going to be losing what little time we still have from our psychiatric social worker, who now has to split herself between this and seven other schools. There was a time when we had enough pupil personnel services —though never really enough—so that we could begin to use a team approach. But that's pie in the sky now, and more kids who need that kind of help are going to slip through. Same with learning disabilities. What we need, what every school needs, is a learning disabilities center. I mean specialists to work with kids on an individual basis and to help me and the classroom teachers plug into how each kid learns best. But there's no chance for that now. Or look at where we are with guidance counselors. We now have only one for the whole school. There should be a guidance counselor for each grade to serve as a liaison between the kids, the parents, the teachers, and any agencies whose help the child or his family might need. All this is basic stuff—if we value children.

"Mind you," Mark Shapiro added, "we're still functioning. We're not giving up. But the frustrations can make you dizzy. For instance, because of the teacher cuts, parents here can no longer freely choose among learning options for their children. In some grades, there are no more openings in the 'traditional' subschool or the open classroom or the bilingual program. Well, find out for yourself what's happening. Look around the school, anywhere you like."

For hours, I sat in on classes, talked to teachers, parents, and kids, and got the clear sense that while Shorackappock—in large part because of Shapiro's leadership—keeps rebounding as best it can after each new assault on its resources, there is welling frustration and, among the adults, anger at those distant decision-makers who keep grinding the school down.

"We used to have a lot of reading programs," a veteran teacher told me, "which let us really focus on the kids individually. They're gone. We don't have the staff. What kinds of values do the people have who do this to us?" I didn't know if she expected an answer. In any case, I had none that would be of any use.

In a second-grade open classroom, I talked to Steve Waring, a remarkably energetic former City College teacher who prefers to work with elementary school kids. His room was cheerily decorated (the multicolored materials paid for by Waring because the school didn't have the money), and the teacher was cracklingly incensed.

Waring fired a rhetorical question: "How can you really be in touch with the independent, individualized work of every single child in an open classroom when your class has been pushed up to thirty-one kids with only a part-time student teacher and, on some days, a marvelous volunteer mother who'll be leaving soon because she's taking her kids out of the public schools and I can't blame her. What's to prevent their deciding we're to have *fifty* kids in a classroom? Or *seventy?* You think that's out of the realm of possibility? Who's to stop them?"

I had become aware of two black-and-white rabbits nibbling at my shoes. Waring looked down and laughed. "No reflection on the administration of this school," he said, "but who do you suppose pays for the rabbits' food and for the things the kids work on for crafts? A lot of teachers, not only me, pay for these extras. But we can't pay for what's really needed—more teachers! I tell you, if there are any more layoffs, I want to be in that group, because I don't want to be standing in a classroom with a whip and a whistle. Do you know what I'd like to have happen? I'd like the mayor and the governor and all the legislators to take turns spending a month with me in this classroom so that they might finally begin to understand priorities. Two weeks would do. Who do you think will be the first to volunteer?"

On the floor above, I met a young science teacher in the bilingual program who, last year, had set up several science clubs for the kids as well as a laboratory. Now, he said morosely, the clubs are gone and the lab is shut. "That may not sound like much to you," he said, "but it all adds up. Or down. Official deprivation is what it is. They just keep cutting down on these kids' chances. And the kids know it. They can figure out how dispensable they are."

Other teachers told me of the disappearance of what they and many parents had regarded as an exceptionally helpful after-school program involving remedial reading and math as well as arts, crafts, games, and sports. "The kids," a math teacher said, "had a place to go besides the streets, and the atmosphere was such that they really looked forward to learning, even after school. Another thing that's gone is the parent education program. There are a lot of Spanish-speaking mothers who are not used to being active in school affairs, to having a real say in what happens to their children. That kind of participation is not in their tradition. So we had a family worker to get them more involved in the school and also to get them into learning English as a second language. There were also parent workshops where they learned how to sew their own clothes to save money and how to help their children with their homework. That's all been cut."

Shorackappock still does have a parents' room, next to the lunchroom, and I went there to see the co-presidents of the parents' association, Peg Dunleavey and Mary Waters. Both are white, both were born and raised in Manhattan, both resist the notion of moving to the suburbs, and both are dismayed at what is happening to their school.

"The open classroom program has been decimated," Peg Dunleavey, a slender, animated woman, said. "And all the way down the line, the cuts have been so disheartening. Why, last year the parents' association presented the school with a thousand dollars' worth of gym equipment. The children were so delighted. But this year we have no gym teacher, so there's no gym program. And we got printing equipment from the Board of Education. But there's nobody, any longer, to show the children how to use it. So that equipment is locked away, as are all kinds of special reading materials because, as a result of the cuts, we don't have a reading teacher in one spot where all those materials can be permanently set up."

Mary Waters, a soft-spoken, kindly woman of firm views, looked at me as her co-president was speaking and finally said, "What do you think it is? Those people who decide about the cuts—is it that they really don't care about our kids? It's so hard to understand, otherwise, what they're doing. I was watching the mayor of Newark on television the other Sunday and he was talking about the cuts he has to make in services for that city. But that mayor said he was not making any cuts in education. That mayor is black and he lives in that city and he cares about the kids in that city. But most of the people who are hurting our kids—they don't even live in New York City. I mean the members of the state legislature and the bankers and industrialists on the State. Emergency Financial Control Board who also determine how much the city can spend, and on what. *Their* kids go to school in the suburbs. And yet they're deciding the future of *our* kids. Even when there's no fiscal emergency in the city, and the bankers and industrialists don't have that power, decisions are still made about our kids from way outside—from the state capital. What can they know about our kids?"

Later that day, I asked the principal his reactions to what the co-presidents of the parents' association had said. I also asked him if he thought the low budget allocations went along with the possible low expectations the budget-makers have of a city school population that is increasingly black and Spanish-speaking.

Mark Shapiro thought awhile and said, "I don't really know if it's a question of low expectations. It may be another kind of prejudice. It's not necessarily that they believe that poor kids, especially black and Spanish-speaking kids, can't do as well as white kids. It's that they're not particularly interested in helping them to do so."

"Why?" I asked.

"Racism, of course," the principal said. "They don't see these kids as *their* kids, as kids for whom they have a visceral sense of responsibility, the kind that Kenneth Gibson feels for the kids of Newark. That could be what it's about. You didn't suppose that racism was no longer a powerful force in this society, did you?"

Whatever the cause of the blight that has stricken New York's and other cities' public schools, no one I spoke to at this elementary school had any clear idea of how to prevent further cuts, let alone repair the damage already done.

"I'm no admirer of Albert Shanker, the head of the teachers' union," said one of the dwindling number of younger teachers at the school, "but at least he's been very outspoken about all of this. Yet as powerful as the United Federation of Teachers is supposed to be, he's not been able to turn it around. As for the parents, most of them are so caught up in just keeping themselves and their kids fed that they have no time to get involved in any kind of sustained organized protest. And if they do have a chance to think about anything as large, as intricate, as how to solve this problem, they feel just plain impotent, like you and me."

"Maybe our only hope," Mary Waters of the parents' association told me, "is to form a children's union. As the Lord said, 'And a child shall lead them.' Maybe we can get a first-grader." She did not sound at all hopeful as she said this.

"But you know," Mary Waters continued, brightening, "some people still do care. Some of the teachers who were let go, for instance, keep coming back. There's one who had a child in her fifth-grade class last year who needed special help, and do you know that woman is here every Tuesday and Thursday morning to continue helping that child? And another teacher, who has found a job with a book company, also can't stay away.

She doesn't want her last year's first-grade children to feel she's abandoned them, and so she keeps bringing in books and sending them all kinds of reading materials. She was just a marvelous teacher. So were most of the others who were laid off. We lost, because of the seniority rules, extraordinarily committed teachers. Young teachers, black and Hispanic teachers. Teachers who would come in at seven-thirty or eight in the morning and stay until five or six. It's sad, it really is. Those people in charge of the money, whoever they are, they don't give a damn about our kids, do they?"

Meanwhile in Inwood, one key school figure in the neighborhood has given up hope. Benjamin Eilbott, principal of P.S. 28 for five years (and an assistant principal for seven years before that), was perhaps the most respected school official throughout the district. Just before Christmas 1975, Eilbott wrote to the parents of the children in his school that he had decided to resign "after months of having to accept a steadily increasing reduction of all vital educational services, and living with what I believe to be the most serious threat ever to the education of children. . . . It was no longer possible for me to be the kind of principal I wished to be."

I knew that many parents and other principals had tried to persuade Eilbott to change his mind. I asked him why he persisted in his decision despite the evident pain it caused him. "My resignation became irrevocable," Eilbott told me, "once I came to the conclusion that this threat to the children was not going to be turned around, that nobody with the power to turn it around was interested in stopping the deterioration of the schools. It would have been dishonest for me to stay because I could not have delivered what should be delivered to these children."

At Shorackappock, Mark Shapiro was greatly disturbed by his colleague's resignation, but Shapiro is not ready to follow him. "So long as I know in my head and in my heart," Shapiro says, "that I'm not causing that deterioration and that I'm doing as much as I can to keep this school a viable institution, I'm not going to let these cuts and what they represent push me out. Sure, there may come a point of no return where I'll feel what Ben is feeling. It could get that bad."

The parents and staff members I spoke to were manifestly relieved that Mark Shapiro is going to stick it out. "In only four years," one of the parents told me, "he's done so much for the school. For one thing, he's *available*. I think I saw his predecessor twice—once in an assembly and once at the top of the stairs reprimanding children who were making noise. Mark is all over the school, his door is always open, and I think he knows every child, from kindergarten on, by name. Almost as soon as the school year starts, he visits each kindergarten class, and then they come visit him, so that a principal doesn't become a frightening thing to these five-year-olds."

"You know," a teacher in the bilingual program added, "when I first came here five years ago, there was not one person on the staff who spoke Spanish although nearly half the kids were Spanish-speaking. So Mark built the bilingual program and set the kind of tone that has led to almost everyone, even the secretaries, wanting to learn Spanish. It's a whole other ball game. Until the cuts, Mark had one of the best open classroom programs in the city, and he pushed our affiliation with City College so that we had a large supply of student teachers. And the parents—the other principal seemed to make it a policy to ignore them. Mark lets them know everything that's going on. In this school you see parents who feel they belong here."

A woman in her thirties, with two children in the open classroom subschool, nodded. "I thought I finally could relax," she said. "I didn't have to worry about schools anymore. And I didn't have to worry about where I was going to get the money for private school. By God, my kids were in the public school to which they were entitled, and it was *better* than private school because it was bilingual. But now I just don't know."

"You're going to pull the kids out?" another woman asked her.

"Oh not right away," she said. "Maybe not at all. But when will the time come when even Mark will have had it with these damn cuts? What's going on is so crazy. Why aren't the parents tearing down the walls of City Hall?"

In the hall outside the principal's office, Perla Sanchez, a lithe, vigorous, red-haired Cuban who is bilingual coordinator at Shorackappock, reacted to our conversation. "Whatever happens," she said, "I am not going to let any of this keep me down. If I give up, what's going to happen to these children? But it *is* crazy, what's going on. What is left of the middle class is going to leave this city. And businesses are going to leave because if the cuts go on and on, who is going to have the skills to work in those businesses? Is that what the people in charge want—to make this city one big ghetto?"

No one answered her. And two third-graders, walking by, looked into the open door of the principal's office, yelled, "Hi, Mr. Shapiro," and strolled on.

Perla Sanchez looked after them. "No, nothing's going to get me out of here."

"Until you're laid off," said one of her more mordant colleagues.

Around the time I was responding to Mark Shapiro's invitation to write about who killed Shorackappock (among other schools), Paul Cowan was describing in the *Village Voice* the equally dismaying effects of budget cuts on another school. In the course of his article, Cowan interviewed a teacher whom we both know, an uncommonly skilled, energetic woman who had intended to spend her life helping kids find and fulfill their potential. And she is tough. In years past, I had watched her successfully battle grimly obtuse principals, school boards, and more than once, the whole Board of Education.

In recent years, however, as education has become less and less of a concern to those running the city, this teacher has become less resilient, less convinced that, long as the odds are, she and the children with whom she is so involved will eventually prevail.

Finally, at the start of 1976, she told Paul Cowan: "The budget cuts have wiped out all the programs we tried to create. I'd be lying to myself if I said I had to stay here and fight. I don't think we've changed anything at all. At this point I'd rather be sitting behind a typewriter or waitressing than listening to the sound of thirty-four kids, wanting. When you spend seven years giving and giving and giving, you begin to feel very selfish. Look, the Board of Education isn't fighting for us. The people outside the schools don't care about us. Try to go to a party and say you're a third-grade teacher. That's a real conversation-stopper."

I have had similar conversations with teachers in New York and in other cities—teachers with a true calling who eventually have come to the conclusion that nobody out here cares about them, and that without support, there isn't that much they can do about thirty-four kids, wanting.

On the other hand, there are teachers, and principals, who won't quit—Perla Sanchez and Mark Shapiro at Shorackappock, among them. But many of them, too, are greatly discouraged at the silence out here, the lack of concerted outrage at what is happening to and in the schools.

At the end of his *Village Voice* article on the mugging of the public schools, Paul Cowan wrote:

Maybe the situation hasn't reached the point where it is luridly dramatic enough for the political activists. How else do you explain the fact that the antiwar movement could persuade 100,000 people to protest the napalming of children in Vietnam, that Right to Lifers can inspire 50,000 people to demonstrate on behalf of fetuses, but there are rarely more than one or two thousand people who will come to a rally for the school children who are being abandoned in New York City . . . ?

And not only in New York City.

Long before the deadening budget cuts of the mid-1970s, schoolchildren were being abandoned. At the beginning of this chapter, I cited Michael Rebell's findings that of the black and Hispanic students who entered the ninth grade of the New York City public school system in 1967, only 51.1 percent of the former and 44.8 percent of the latter were still enrolled four years later. Harvey Scribner, former chancellor of the city's school system, cites a later study by the Citizens' Committee for Children which reveals that of *all* the kids who entered New York City high schools as the class of 1968, at least a third had dropped out before graduation.

In his book, *Make Your Schools Work* (written with Leonard Stevens), Scribner makes a basic, troubling point in the form of a question: "If one third of the lights in New York City went off, if one third of the subway system stopped running, if one third of the stores decided to leave the city, there would be a public uproar and massive official action."

But when one-third (and more) of the city's high school students are turned off and out, there is no citizen uproar, no official action to at least try to repair the damage. Nobody at the Board of Education, or in any other public office, even knows where they've gone. Or cares.

In 1974, on their way to high school, 87 percent of the elementary and junior high school students in Harlem failed the standardized reading tests. There was no citizen uproar about that chilling augury either.

Nor can there be, of course, says Harvey Scribner, "until these facts shame us."

The Fallen Chancellor

At this point in the book, looking ahead, I draw on two of the more stubbornly resourceful educators I have known through the years. One, Harvey Scribner, was a political failure in the most important position of his career—the chancellorship of the New York public school system. That is, he couldn't keep the job. Yet the reasons for his failure have considerable value for the future, and much of Scribner's own basic approach to learning is central to the future of education, even though he wasn't able to stay long enough in New York City to sufficiently prepare the soil so that his ideas could become deeply enough rooted.

The second of these battlers against the child-compressors inside the schools, as he tries to organize support forces outside the walls, is Elliott Shapiro. He occasionally considers himself somewhat of a failure, although he has strongly influenced thousands of teachers throughout the country, as well as a good many administrators. What he has learned, through decades of showing others how to learn and teach, is also important to the future of the public schools.

Elliott Shapiro, who was a community superintendent of schools (one of thirty-two in New York) while Harvey Scribner was chancellor, was not much impressed with the chancellor. "He is not leading," Shapiro would complain to me about Scribner. "What a forum he has, head of the whole school system. And he's not leading."

I used to try to defend Scribner, pointing out the persistent public onslaughts the chancellor was making against the dreadnoughts of the entrenched past. "He's shaking up the whole system," I'd tell Shapiro. "That's leadership."

"Not if you do it all alone," Shapiro said. "That's not leading. That's being foolhardy. And Scribner is so busy fighting his enemies in the system, he hasn't even begun to organize a rank-and-file coalition of teachers and parents that could really turn things around, create an acute public awareness of our needs, finally bring the schools out of isolation and into the very center of the community where they belong. *That's* leadership."

Shapiro turned out to be right in that Scribner had indeed been foolhardy in going into combat as a loner against massed institutional forces. Yet Scribner also did exercise leadership— in terms of the ideas he kept trying to propel into public discourse. The ideas couldn't save him, but an account of his odyssey can be of considerable value to future paladins of children —and to the parents of those children.

Educationally, Scribner was right—for New York and for all other cities. Politically, he flunked.

Dr. Harvey Scribner, a plain-spoken native of Maine with a passion for enabling people to learn, took office as chancellor of New York City's enormous, underfinanced, and under-achieving public school system on September 1, 1970. His first two years were exceptionally difficult, involving him, he once told me, in far too many hours of argument with adults about adults' problems when he would much rather have spent more of his time in the schools. The arguments were inevitable, however, because the chancellor made his intentions about school reform clear from the start, and to many of the system's professional staff members those intentions came through as an indictment of past practices. And so they were intended. A month after taking office, Scribner, in a speech before the city's Public Education Association—his remarks were later printed as an unprecedentedly subversive special supplement to the school system's "Staff Bulletin"—said that any reform of the schools "must proceed from the premise that the condition of public education today is intolerable," and that the schools "have drummed the self-respect from many of our children, and stifled the rest under layers of rigid rules and inflexible policies." In mid-November of 1970, addressing the Metropolitan Conference of B'nai B'rith, the chancellor was somewhat more specific about what he was up to. "We ought to question every system which we have built into the schools: systems of staff selection and promotion, systems of curriculum organization, systems of responsibility and accountability," he said. "The measure should be whether a system serves kids, or itself."

A frequent criticism of the chancellor during this early period, and for the rest of his first year, was that while he was quick to list the failures of the schools, he offered no solutions. He invariably answered that if there was to be change, it would be effective and durable only if it came from below—from students and teachers and members of the city's thirty-two locally elected community school boards. "I can try to set the tone, the spirit," Scribner said at that time, "but no one man is going to make a breakthrough. Nor is a small staff in the chancellor's office ever going to be able to run this system. We have to find and encourage enough people out there who are sympathetic to our programs and give these people whatever support we can as they work the programs out. Any real restructuring of this system is going to have to be done from the bottom up."

Nonetheless, Scribner, during his first year, started his own staff members—some of whom were young people he had recruited from outside the system—exploring alternatives to established practices. How could the huge high schools be broken up, both inside the building and outside, by means of individual learning options? Was it necessary to keep planning—and waiting for—large school buildings, or were there better, cheaper, smaller spaces for learning in the city? If something new was working well in one classroom, how could teachers, principals, and community boards throughout the city most effectively learn about it and evaluate it for themselves? Whenever I saw the chancellor in his office, in the Board of Education building at 110 Livingston Street in Brooklyn, these projects were what he was most interested in talking about. On some days he was quite hopeful, and on others he felt himself sinking into the frustration that had swallowed up others who have tried to deal with what one Scribner staff assistant calls "the octopus."

A few days after Christmas of his first year, Scribner, with an unusually sharp edge to his Yankee twang, said to me, "I don't think people have any idea of how tough it is for anyone trying to run a big city school system to get a handle on anything. One hour, I think I'm getting a sense of control—seeing where I might be able to connect some of these ideas we're examining so they'll have a chance of working. And an hour later I don't feel I have a handle on anything. It's as if I were at the bottom of a well, just looking up at the sky. But I'll get there. Bit by bit. You see, all my life I've been what I call a ten-percenter. That's a pretty good interest rate—isn't it?—if you have a million dollars to invest. In education, if we can make a 10 percent change for some of the kids tomorrow morning, or next month, we ought to do it. And if we keep making a 10 percent difference in other places in the system, we'll eventually be getting some real gain. I don't hold with waiting for the day of utopia, when, all of a sudden, the whole system will have been changed."

I asked the chancellor how much time he thought he would have to add up his returns on his present job. Some of the older professionals throughout the system were convinced, as the chancellor knew, that in his first few months in office he had become too controversial to survive for more than a year of his three-year contract. And the mayor, John Lindsay, had told me a few weeks before, "I admire Scribner and what he's trying to do, but I wonder if he can make it. The only people who have been able to last in that kind of job are politicians, and that he's not."

"Oh, I don't worry about survival," Scribner said. "I live day to day." (O.K. as a philosophy affecting Scribner himself, I thought, but as chancellor he was responsible for a lot more than his own survival; and if he was expunged, all the rest of what he had tried to build would probably go down with him.)

Almost from the beginning of his term there were indeed intermittent demands that the chancellor be fired, or resign. They came from leaders of the Elementary School Principals Association and from members of the Council of Supervisors and Administrators, which includes high school principals. And Albert Shanker, the president of the United Federation of Teachers (he has since also become president of the American Federation of Teachers), warned four months after Scribner took office that unless the chancellor changed his direction very quickly, "his days in New York City as Chancellor are numbered."

Though these critics took issue with the chancellor on many counts—his including students on committees of advisers in the selection of high school principals, for instance—spokesmen for both the teachers and the supervisors were in most serious conflict with him over how decentralized the city's school system was going to be. In 1969, the New York State Legislature passed a law decentralizing New York City's schools by providing for thirty-one (later thirty-two) locally elected boards. Scribner saw that measure as having "set in motion a plan to bring educational decision-making and school management substantially closer to the people for whom the public schools were created and who are the schools' ultimate owners." It was, he said, "an extraordinarily important piece of legislation, imperfect as it is, because decentralization is about the only hope we have of making urban education work."

If Scribner had only *said* such things, the system's professional staff could bear the rhetoric. But from the beginning he was actively working toward giving the community school boards greater flexibility in the hiring and firing of teachers and administrative personnel. If the local boards were to obtain more such powers, more professional staff members would become directly accountable to "the schools' ultimate owners" —a prospect that makes many teachers and supervisors uneasy. They strongly doubt, many of them say, whether nonprofessionals know enough about education to judge professionals. And they have a more deeply rooted fear that under decentralization, hiring and firing will be determined by race or by some other factor not related to competence alone.

Scribner replied to these concerns by saying, "Whatever their level of education or sophistication, I have faith that most parents try to do what they believe is right for their kids, and I think the same kind of motivation holds for the community board members. This is not to say that mistakes will not be made, that all boards will invariably make good decisions, simply because they are closer to the people of their district. But who can say that all decisions made at central headquarters are good, or right, or appropriate, or are made without tinge of bias? And there is something to be said for letting the people who have to live with a decision make it."

In furtherance of that desideratum, the chancellor also recommended that each community board prepare criteria based on the specific educational needs of its district as additional standards for the employment and promotion of its staff.

"If we can get this going, not only will the community boards have access to the widest possible pool of talent, but they'll be able to function more effectively, too," Scribner told me one day. "In order to help set up performance criteria, you, as a community board member, will have to be as specific as possible about what you think the purposes of education in your district ought to be. At the end of a specified period, you will be able to evaluate a teacher by how well he has fulfilled those purposes. You can't, after all, hold teachers accountable until you've made it clear what you expect of them. We're long past the notion, or should be, that they are primarily required to be neat and prompt, and to remember to keep the temperature at seventy-two degrees and the window shades at the proper level. Setting criteria for the staff in each district can finally, and fairly, alter the tradition that a teacher is guaranteed his job for life, no matter how he performs. The way it is now in this city, and many others, you've got more than a 99 percent chance of surviving your probationary period and making tenure. And once you make tenure, you've got an even better chance of staying on as long as you want to. Obviously, that kind of system doesn't do much for the learning needs of kids. It serves the requirements of adults. Ewald Nyquist, the state commissioner of education, has said—and I've quoted him many times—'The probationary period of the teacher belongs to the child.' That is, it should belong to the child." Scribner also advocated that teachers have their licenses and tenure reviewed periodically, on the basis of what they have actually achieved with their students, "to ensure continued competence."

Such insistence that teachers actually be accountable for their failures, even unto possibly losing their jobs, made Scribner even more controversial during the last half of his first year than during its gusty opening months. A young assistant to Scribner told me one morning, "This is the kind of day on which, after reading the papers, I have to get out the list of all the 'alternative learning' projects we're working on in order to be able to keep going. A lot of this stuff—like finding new learning space, and what's going to be happening in some of the high schools this fall—is news. But the press isn't interested in that. If you go by the papers, all Scribner ever does is get into fights. I'm not worried about him. He keeps coming back. But as for what we're really into around here, I'd like to see a good guy win for once."

Scribner, however, was quite cheerful that morning. "I'm hearing from more and more people deep down in the system," he said. "Teachers and students. I think they know why I'm here."

One of the people he had heard from was a fifteen-year-old high school sophomore, who had written the chancellor a letter in mid-February. Her father was a principal in the city system. "Going to school is something that becomes more and more tiresome each day, and I must admit to waking up early on school mornings and not being able to go back to sleep because the misery of knowing that the precious day will be spent in school keeps me up brooding," she wrote. "I enjoy learning, I look forward to making personal discoveries in my everyday life, and I've found school hindering me from doing so, and also, more important is that sometimes they've made me feel that my personal discoveries about life, people and our complex world are not worth discovering. I've even begun to feel guilty at times when writing a poem instead of studying for a test. It is ironic, and unfortunately truthfully sad." The girl added that she had become aware of certain educators, Scribner among them, who were "enlightened and passionate about getting changes done." What now kept her going, she went on, was the knowledge that "the chancellor of the schools is on my side. That someone, other than myself, realizes that life is in reality a perpetual learning process." She concluded, "I see now that I don't stand alone believing these seemingly rebellious thoughts."

The chancellor was unable to reach the girl by phone, so he wrote her a note, saying, "I receive a good deal of personal correspondence from people who either agree or disagree with my positions or statements, but your letter is one-of-a-kind. Because it is from a student, because it displays such sensitivity, and because it shows such hope for a better future your letter has lifted my spirits immeasurably. You have let me know that I, too, do not stand alone in holding to these 'rebellious thoughts,' and that is good to know, especially when I realize that people like you are willing to stand with me. I wish you well. May you learn not to feel guilty when writing a poem, and may your learning continue long after you leave school."

The chancellor's most fervent hope for anyone in school anywhere is that the desire to learn not stop with schooling—that pleasure in learning not be blunted or destroyed by schooling. He had firsthand experience of how discouraging school can be, and although he overcame that sense of defeat, he remembers how long the odds against him were at the time. Scribner, who was born in Albion, Maine, grew up in poverty in a broken home. "I was a failure in school, a total failure," he told me one day. "School was just not a meaningful place to me. I got out of high school at fifteen. They hustled me through because they were awfully glad to see me go. I spent the next couple of years on Matinicus Isle, off Rockland, where I delivered coal and groceries for a fellow who owned a store. I sort of began getting an education there, just through doing and seeing different things. Somehow, I decided to train to be a teacher. I don't know what turned me on, but I do remember the day I told my mother, 'Ma, I've decided to go to college.' Her immediate reaction was 'Don't be a damn fool, Harvey.' It was impossible. Nobody in our family had even talked about going to college."

Scribner followed his calling, however, and it proved to be a true one. After working as a teacher, a principal, and a superintendent of schools in Maine and Massachusetts—earning degrees all the while, including a bachelor of arts from Farmington State Teachers College in Maine and a doctorate at Boston University—he headed the schools of Teaneck, New

Jersey, through most of the 1960s. There he became successfully involved in a battle to integrate the school system. From
1968 to the time the Board of Education appointed him New
York City's chancellor, Scribner was the resolutely innovative
commissioner of education in Vermont. Later, he liked to give
visitors to his office at New York's Board of Education a copy
of a lively, amiably illustrated pamphlet titled "Vermont Design for Education," which he helped develop. It's full of such
apothegms as these:

> Education should be based upon the individual's strong, in-
> herent desire to learn and to make sense of his environ-
> ment. . . .

> Education should strive to maintain the individuality and
> originality of the learner. The school's function is to expand
> the differences between individuals and create a respect for
> those differences. . . .

> A school situation should be flexible and divergent enough to
> allow each person regularly to find some measure of success.
> . . . All people need success to prosper. Youth is no exception.

Scribner knew too much about schools, however, to have any
faith in the power of pieties alone to move systems and the
people in them. Accordingly, as chancellor, he worked long
hours and read a great deal, almost entirely books on education, trying to match theories and desires with what was actually being done in a particular school, a particular classroom.
Nearly every time I saw him during those years, Scribner asked
me whether I had read or heard of a certain book and whether
anything I was reading currently might be of use to him. At one
time, he was enthusiastically recommending *Homework,* a
book by Gloria Channon, who has been a teacher in New York
City's schools for more than a decade. The book described ways
in which she had been learning to make both her classroom and

herself more open to learning. As soon as Scribner had finished the book, he asked to see Mrs. Channon, and they met at his office. Knowing her and having read her book and her magazine articles on schools, I asked Mrs. Channon for her appraisal of the chancellor.

"In Buber's terms, he's a very I-Thou person," she said. "Since the school system is awash with I-Its, this creates quite a problem in communication. In my visit, I found him very open in his feelings, very direct, and a fantastic brain-picker. Also, he seems to have made the leap to the top without losing the knowledge of what it's like to be a teacher. Most people forget what the classroom is like as soon as they become guidance counselors or principals, let alone chancellors. Or maybe they never really knew the classroom except as a place to get out of as soon as possible. He is realistic about the classroom, and he is also completely realistic about the power structure in the system, including the inertia working against him. I think the system underestimates him, but I don't know how much of an impact he's actually going to have. If he can get through to enough of us fast enough—maybe, maybe, maybe. I'd love to see him call meetings for all the teachers, district by district, and talk with them. He is hard to resist. I know that I had sort of closed myself up in my own classroom—periodic withdrawals to lick my wounds seem to be my style—and had given up trying to influence change in even one school. Just so they let me alone. But after I met with him I went back to school with the feeling that I owed it to him and myself and the kids to start in again, to go once more through the long, dull, dreary process of fighting the Jell-O monster, the system, in the hope that this time, with ol' Harv up there cheering me on, I might make a dent in it."

The chancellor was still optimistic about his own chances against the Jell-O monster when I next saw him, a week before school started in September of 1971. He had worked straight through the summer. "I did take off a couple of Fridays and a couple of Mondays," he said, his feet on his desk, "but I didn't want to be too far away because I'm finally getting a pretty good feeling of where I am in this job and where I want to go. Last year was the year for asking questions. This year, we have to start delivering."

And that fall a number of the projects initiated by Scribner and his staff began to take palpable form. And other alternative learning plans—some of which had come from teachers and students within the system—were becoming manifest. On the opening day of school in his second year, for example, the chancellor spent part of the morning looking over the new "mini-schools" at Haaren High School, on Manhattan's West Side. In recent years, the school, with an enrollment of 2,500 students, had had high dropout and truancy rates. Now an idea worked out by some Haaren students and faculty members and speedily implemented by Scribner and his staff had resulted in the division of Haaren into twelve mini-schools, each of them in its own area of the building and most of them accommodating fewer than two hundred students. Each of these schools-within-a-school was based on a different theme, around which all its courses were designed. The themes, or identities, ranged from "College Bound," "Aviation," and "Pre Tech" to "Careers" and "Special Education."

"There's still a lot to be done to make the mini-school concept and other alternative learning plans work," Scribner said later that year, "but if we succeed we'll have shown that we can begin to close the gap between students and teachers. A high school with an enrollment of thousands of students, for instance, does not have to be impersonal. And we'll have learned more about how best to provide learning options—a range of learning experiences that can relate to many different kinds of kids, connecting with where they are and where they want to go."

Scribner, in the course of his term, persuaded the Rockefeller Brothers Fund to supply an initial fifty-thousand-dollar grant, with which he started a Learning Cooperative in the fall of 1971. Afterward, additional funds were secured from other foundations as well as from federal, state, and city sources. One of the cooperative's functions was to identify significant programs in the schools and to spread the news about them to other districts. It also served to set up links between college-based teacher-training programs and individual schools and teachers in the city system. "We've got to find ways to position the center of gravity of teacher education *in the public schools,* not in the colleges—both for those who want to be teachers and for those already teaching," Scribner emphasized. "The former need training in reality, and the latter need to be able to leave their regular responsibilities from time to time so that they can keep learning about teaching. We've got to put an end to the notion that pre-service and in-service programs are separate entities. And we can do it by creating a continuous flow between the colleges and the classrooms."

In addition, the Learning Cooperative was to work with the thirty-two local school districts while also establishing centers around the city that would link schools with businesses, industries, government agencies, and museums in order to increase children's learning experiences outside a school building and also to find them part-time, paying jobs they could fill while still attending school.

This last direction, expanding and varying the places in which students learn, was one that especially interested Scribner. He is convinced that fundamental rethinking is necessary concerning the nature and purpose of space for education. "We've trained the public to believe that there is some direct relationship between good education and a fancy building. There isn't," he says. "And when there's overcrowding, ought we to keep thinking only in terms of constructing new buildings? I don't think so. We're looking into more extensive use of leased space. If we can lease smaller units of space throughout the city, it will be easy to organize smaller groups of students and to create linkages between the school and the community." Scribner's plan was to find areas in office buildings, lofts, hotels, stores, catering halls, and apartment houses that could be adapted quickly and inexpensively for what he foresaw as "many newly emerging educational programs requiring new varieties of space—some 'open,' some for small groups, some for individual study." The chancellor also believed then, as now, that when the construction of new schools is required, they ought to be smaller schools. In a memorandum he sent the city's community school boards, he pointed out that "small school units of four hundred to six hundred students have great educational advantages, because of the intimacy and attention to all individuals which can be achieved." Furthermore, he noted, "a school of this size can be accommodated comfortably on a site of half an acre, which means that locations can be found with few or no encumbrances."

Before he left New York, Scribner and his staff accumulated a sizable list of other projects and possibilities in various stages of development. He proposed, for instance, that high school dropouts be given credit toward an "external diploma" if they succeed in jobs that the school system and their employers agree on as indicators of achievement in particular skills. "If the idea of high school is to prepare a student for the outside world, and a dropout achieves success in the outside world, then he should be given the credit," Scribner said. "And the stigma of being a dropout would then be removed."

In his office one afternoon during his second year, Scribner, after telling me about his plan for an external diploma, further pursued his favorite theme. "You really have to keep looking hard at this thing called 'education' to find out how many things we keep doing just because we've always done them," he said. "I have another question: Why should a student be able to go to school only between eight in the morning and four in the afternoon? Why not have some high schools that operate from five in the evening until eleven? Why shouldn't some students have the option of keeping their days free, maybe to work? Another question: Why can't some school buildings be used more at night by parents? I'd like to see schools become little city halls at night, where parents could go for everything from community organizing to learning how to play chess or the violin, if they wanted to. And it mightn't be a bad idea if the kids were to involve themselves in helping the parents set up these programs. Alternatives are what I'm after, choices that parents and students can make for themselves. I'd like to see the voucher concept—parents being able to choose the kind of education they want for their children—become part of the public school system. In any given school, why can't we have many different models for learning? Why shouldn't a parent be able to choose from, let's say, seven different approaches to learning in seven different third grades? The classrooms ought to range from a good traditional way of teaching and learning to the most open classroom imaginable. And if you, the parent, felt that the first choice didn't work out for the particular needs of your child, then you ought to be able to change. Not as a privilege, but as part of the normal practice of the school."

Scribner's zeal for finding and cultivating learning choices was emphasized for me a few minutes later when I asked him about curriculum planning. The word *curriculum* clearly offended him. He clamped down on his pipe and said, "I don't much hold with that word unless you're talking about a different curriculum for each child."

It was past five o'clock, and an assistant opened the door. "Can I see you before you leave?" he asked the chancellor.

"What makes you think I'm going to leave?" Scribner answered. "I've got a meeting here tonight, and a lot to do before that."

I rose to go, and as the chancellor walked with me to the door he said, "Well, I'm looking forward to these next months with considerable enthusiasm. There's a myth around that nothing good can happen in the schools this year because we've been hit with the budget cuts. I'm trying to get people to stop crying about that. Sure, we need more money than what we've got, but meanwhile we have to hold ourselves accountable for what we do with what we have. I include myself; I'm not satisfied with my performance so far. I've got to do better. Of course, I always do have a happy dissatisfaction with my performance."

Before leaving the building, I went into an adjoining office to speak to one of Scribner's assistants. "I heard him talking about accountability," the aid said. "That's the way he operates up here. He's always after us for follow-ups—detailed follow-ups. How's this project going? What's holding that one up? Where's the research material I asked for two days ago?" The aid laughed and went on: "The other day, after the chancellor had got one hell of a drubbing on the evening news—from the teachers' union, from a community board member angry about the budget cuts, from a guy in the supervisors' union—I came in feeling that he needed some kind of show of support. So I went into his office and said, 'Chancellor, there are a number of people here who will go through a brick wall for you.' He had a pained look on his face. 'I don't care about that,' he said. 'No, that's not right. I do. Loyalty is fine. But can they deliver?' "

In the months that followed, the chancellor continued to push himself to deliver, and although criticism of him, particularly by the leadership of the United Federation of Teachers, scarcely abated, he still seemed resilient. (That criticism primarily concerned Scribner's persistent efforts to increase the decision-making powers of the local school boards, a move that the union, with its *city-wide* contract, considered threatening to the security of its members.) When I saw him during the third, and final, year of his initial contract, it was clear that he wanted to stay. "Sure, it's murderous," he told me. "I curse and swear and wonder how the hell I ever got myself into this mess, but I like it. I feel much more a part of the system. God, I'd better not say that. I mean that I feel I'm playing much more of a leadership role. By now, the establishment, perhaps reluctantly, accepts the fact that I speak with some weight and that I may not be talking just for the time being—I may be here for a longer period."

"But what if your contract isn't renewed?" I asked.

Scribner leaned back in his chair and said, "My wife and I have always wanted to take a trip. We've never been to Europe, and I especially want to go to Africa. So instead of talking about whether I get fired from this job, to us it's a matter of when we're going to take the trip. Meanwhile I am very much here, and things are moving. We've got more high school learning alternatives going, and through decentralization, more parents are beginning to realize that they can become involved in making decisions about their schools. And as they do, they'll learn, I hope, that they can organize to have great impact on state and federal legislators—not only to get more funds, but also to enable each district to be flexible enough so that more experimentation can take place. For instance, I'd like to see the state legislature create sixty community boards in this city instead of the thirty-two we now have. Then each board would have fewer kids to deal with. And if we're going to have complete decentralization, which I favor, each community board would have greater freedom to initiate the kinds of changes that might best serve the kids in its specific district. Just to begin with, if the community boards are to be accountable to *their* basic constituency, the parents, they should have the right to hire and fire the teachers and supervisors in their own schools, regardless of the changes that would require in the city-wide union contracts."

I mentioned to the chancellor that various critics had said that the present limited system of decentralization, then two years old, had made no appreciable educational difference in the city's elementary and junior high schools.

"That criticism reminds me of the story of the farmer who bought a run-down house with brush growing all around it," Scribner said. "The grass hadn't been cut and the roof was leaking, but in time he really brought it to life and made something out of it. One day, the minister rode by and said, 'Farmer Jones, I've got to tell you that you and God are doing a great job with this farm.' The farmer looked at him and said, 'You should have seen it when God had it all alone.' Well, you should have seen the New York City public school system when the central headquarters had it all alone. Viewed in that context, I think, the local boards have done a hell of a good job. Some are stronger than others, but most have started to get hold of the situation. They know a lot more about the mechanics of the operation. They've learned about the processes of funding, and about how to make the most of what they've got. They have certainly learned a lot about what they are prevented from doing by the teachers' union contract. Now, instead of staying home and grousing, they are part of what is actually going on."

"There's another kind of grousing, to use your term," I said to the chancellor. "During the past two years, many more principals than usual have retired before reaching the mandatory age of seventy. Some of them say your presence has sped their departure."

"It may be that, as one parent said to me, 'it's all for the good,' " Scribner replied. "In any case, one result is that the newer principals are becoming part of my constituency. More important than that, obviously, is their ability to improve their schools. A year ago, five high schools were in terrible shape. These were schools with much violence and frustration. All five —Benjamin Franklin, George Washington, Julia Richman, Port Richmond, and Eastern District—have new principals. They are my appointees. The tensions in those high schools have markedly decreased, and a good deal more learning is going on. I consider that an accomplishment. Another one is developing alternative routes to getting a high school diploma, which I think is the best idea I've had since I've been here. I'm convinced that many kids—not all—can best learn how to learn in places other than schools. This applies to kids who have already dropped out or are in a number of our alternative programs that extend beyond classrooms. Doing real work in city agencies and in other jobs, they can acquire skills that they feel relate to their future—whether that future leads to college or directly into the job market. Not only should they get credit for that kind of learning, but skills gained on the outside should result in a first-class diploma a kid would have received if he had stayed in a classroom in his original high school. What the hell should a high school diploma signify? That you sat at my feet for a given period of time, or that you can perform at certain levels of demonstrated proficiency?

"We're moving toward broadening the definition of education and of where it can take place," Scribner continued. "Not everyone in this city, to be sure, is happy about where we're going. I even get death threats. I guess I've been a week without any from time to time, but I usually get a few each week. Horrible letters. The kind that say, 'We're drawing lots to give you an acid facial.' I remember one in particular: 'I go to church every morning and pray you'll die before night, and I pray that death will come by way of cancer of the throat.' The letters generally focus on something I'm going to try in order to get equality for minority kids. The letter about the acid facial was brought on by my plan for the external diploma. The writer was angry that I wanted to give diplomas to those no-good blacks and Puerto Ricans who weren't sitting still in a classroom. But I am getting more support every day for the idea that we have to beat down this false distinction between learning in a school and learning in the community. That support is coming from parents—and, I'm happy to say, from more principals."

The chancellor and I next talked about the predictions, made soon after he was hired, that he either would soon be caught in the bureaucratic quicksand of the public school system or would be forced out because of his insistence on trying to swing the balance of power in the schools toward those he refers to as the owners and consumers of public education.

"Well, while I can't say I feel a great sense of accomplishment so far, I can also say the situation is not as it was when I came," Scribner told me. "And I have survived so far—on my terms. God knows, it's slow work. A few months ago, I had something to do with persuading two young teachers on the Lower East Side not to bail out of the system, as they were about to do in frustration because of an especially rigid principal. We met, and I asked them to hang on. I told them, 'Those who prefer a static system want people like you to leave. Don't let this happen. Don't fall in with their plans. I know you're having a hard time, but let me tell you about some of my problems. I'd like to think we're all strong enough to hang in together.' So each has switched to a different school, but they're staying in the system. As I intend to."

Scribner, despite his intentions, did not stay in the New York public school system. Pressures for his removal continued and the Board of Education finally succumbed, though deviously. While the board never said publicly that Scribner's contract would not be renewed, its continuing silence on the matter into the third year of Scribner's three-year contract forced the chancellor, as I expect the Board of Education knew would happen, to ask for a clear statement, one way or another, on the renewal. He could not be a "lame duck" chancellor if his program was to continue to develop momentum. The Board of Education, however, preferring not to have the firing of Scribner on its record—for the chancellor did have the support of *The New York Times* and various civic education groups—ignored Scribner's request for a declaration of its intention. Accordingly, Scribner, a proud man, resigned in December 1972. ("I'll walk out of this city with my head held high," Scribner had said a year before, and that he did.)

Essentially a loner, Scribner had not possessed either the inclination or the perspicacity to commit some of his time and energy, from the beginning of his stay as chancellor, to help organize a coalition that would do battle for him and his priorities against the teachers' and supervisors' unions. And so the latter prevailed. There was a considerable potential for a pro-Scribner coalition—among blacks and Puerto Ricans, public education organizations, and not a small number of younger white parents who very much agreed with Scribner's plans to provide a sizable range of learning alternatives in the schools. But these sectors of the public never coalesced because no one had made clear to them soon enough that Scribner could not survive as a paladin for children with only a small group of his assistants behind him. That is, he could not survive without organized counterpower in a large city in which the two groups that he insisted had to be made accountable for the quality of education—the teachers and the supervisors—were most efficiently organized against *him*.

Harvey Scribner went on to become a professor of education at the University of Massachusetts, where he now inculcates future teachers, principals, and administrators with the ideas he started to institute in the New York City schools.

In its farewell to Scribner, *The New York Times* proclaimed editorially that Scribner had "approached an excruciatingly difficult mission with common sense and an open mind toward change." The *Times* also predicted that Scribner's truncated term as chancellor was "certain to win eventual applause and appreciation as a brave effort in the school system's search for a new beginning."

Perhaps. It depends on which way the public school systems in New York and other cities go. Not that they would have to be "revolutionized" for Scribner's New York defeat to be redeemed. Scribner is not, and never was, that much of a radical. He is an unremitting reformer. For further example, all of his often fierce criticisms of the public schools are based on his devout belief in their perfectibility. Unlike such truly woolly radicals as Ivan Illich, Scribner has never thought of doing away with the whole notion of compulsory public schooling up to a certain age. In fact, when the National Commission on the Reform of Secondary Education decided a while ago that "forced schooling" is "the foremost problem in American education"—and recommended that students be allowed to leave school at fourteen, two years earlier than the permissible leave-taking age in most states—Scribner exploded.

In his book, *Make Your Schools Work,* the former chancellor asked sharply:

> One wonders to whom the Commission spoke. Did the people who live in the central Harlems and the Appalachias . . . say that "forced schooling" is the "foremost problem" with their schools? Did they say that if their fourteen-year-old sons and daughters were allowed to leave school, their lives would be enhanced? Did the Commission not see that non-compulsory education requires a positive alternative, a place to go; and that lacking a place to go, the kind of recommendation it put forth would not liberate the young, but would free the schools to rid themselves systematically and legally of the particularly "troublesome" students who learn slowly and behave badly—the "dull" and the "maladjusted" who "get in the way" of the majority?

Actually Scribner, although he agrees with much in the revisionist histories of American education, still believes in the power of schooling to transform a life. If schools were made smaller, if there were more learning options, if the consumers of education and their parents had more deciding power, if teachers were judged on the basis of how effectively they taught rather than on what courses they took to get the job—then schooling could work for just about everybody. What could be more sensible? Not, however, to the massed teachers' and supervisors' unions, who could not abide the subversive notion that they be held responsible for the quality of their work. And so there came to be the chancellor's defenestration.

The Visiting Professor
from the Real World

In the spring of 1972, the year in which Harvey Scribner was forced to leave New York, Dr. Elliott Shapiro, after thirty-five years in the New York City public school system, retired. At the time he was community superintendent of District 2, which encompasses two-fifths of the borough of Manhattan, stretching from the Lower East Side to 96th Street and including, on the West Side, Chinatown, Greenwich Village, the Chelsea-Clinton area, and the Lincoln Center neighborhood. Once, more than once, Shapiro had wanted to head the whole school system, but he never thought he had much of a chance. He was right.

I had first met Elliott Shapiro, as I noted before, in the early 1960s, when he was principal of P.S. 119, a lively elementary school in central Harlem. Since his concern for the children insistently extended to their lives outside of school, Dr. Shapiro knew many of their families and often served as an effective prod to city agencies to whom housing and other complaints had been previously made without response. Long before the term was in official use in the New York school hierarchy, Shapiro was a true *community* schoolman.

Along with a large and persistent parents' association,

Shapiro and his staff, moreover, were particularly engaged during that period in Harlem in fighting for a new school. In 1961, for instance, in a move unprecedented in the history of the New York public schools, P.S. 119's staff placed an ad in the now-defunct *World-Telegram* listing in appalling detail—from the prevalence of rats and roaches to sagging walls and unsanitary children's toilets—the dangerous deterioration of their bleak, fortresslike school building, which had been erected in 1899.

That ad, and a resultant visit to the school by Mayor Robert Wagner—who encountered a rat during his tour—put Dr. Shapiro in disfavor at the Board of Education. "Elly," an associate superintendent had said to him, "why didn't you go through channels? This is a hell of a thing—airing our dirty linen in public. You're disgracing us!" It was hardly the first time Dr. Shapiro had annoyed the school system's hierarchy, but as he kept emphasizing, "My loyalty is to the children rather than to any institution." (He is one of the relatively few people I know who can say that without sounding treacly, because he knows what he's actually done.)

In 1966, a new building, P.S. 92, took the place of P.S. 119, and Dr. Shapiro remained principal for one more term before spending a year in the Rochester public school system as head of the Center for Cooperative Action for Urban Education. There he helped initiate and get considerable federal funding for some dozen projects aimed at keeping kids in school who might otherwise, as Luther Seabrook puts it, have slipped through the system. Dr. Shapiro returned to New York in 1967 as superintendent of what was then District 3; and in 1970, after a remapping of the city's school district lines, he was elected community superintendent by the local school board of District 2.

From time to time, in recent years, I have looked in on Dr. Shapiro to learn something of what he has been learning in his various positions in the public school system and in his post-retirement teaching of those who want to move ahead in that

system. These conversations have taken place in his community superintendent's office at P.S. 116 on East 33rd Street; at
his Peter Cooper Village apartment overlooking, much to his
pleasure, a playground; and in his fifteenth-floor office at Yeshiva University on lower Fifth Avenue. Dr. Shapiro's notion
of retirement was to accept a full-time appointment as visiting
professor of school administration and supervision in that university's Ferkauf Graduate School of Humanities and Social
Sciences.

During one of these visits at Yeshiva, I arrived a couple of
hours before Shapiro was to teach a class in educational leadership. His students, many already working in the school systems
of New York City and the surrounding area, are studying for
their doctorates, which, they hope, will lead to administrative
and other supervisory positions in the schools.

A recurring subject of our conversations during the past few
years has been "accountability," a term increasingly in vogue
throughout the country, but so far much more discussed than
put to any real test. When a child fails to learn, the concept
goes, there has to be a way to measure the degree to which both
teachers and supervisors are accountable for that failure. But
what *are* the ways? And what if teachers and administrators,
for instance, do not want to be made accountable in the ways
in which school boards or parents think they should be judged?
Who decides?

As I walked into his office, Dr. Shapiro was on the phone
arranging a meeting with a student working on his doctoral
dissertation. Tall, slightly stoop-shouldered, his eyeglasses
pushed back on thinning white hair, and his features resem-
bling those of a tired but alert eagle, Dr. Shapiro waved me to
a seat as he finished his telephone conversation.

"I've been doing some more thinking about accountability,"
he told me. "It seems to me that a school's staff has to be
measured not only with regard to the quality of the teaching
and the efficiency of the administration, but also with respect

to that school's involvement in the living conditions of its neighborhood, the neighborhood the children come from. If you're really saying that education has to deal with 'the whole child,' then teachers and administrators in a poverty area, for instance, ought to be knowledgeable about the disasters that often take place in the lives of poor people. If a school isn't involved in the family's housing problems and in the quality of health services the family gets, then that school should get a negative accountability rating."

As a specific example of this kind of school accountability, Dr. Shapiro told me how a serious drug problem at Charles Evans Hughes High School in Manhattan had been handled when he was community superintendent of District 3. With money provided by the Rockefeller Brothers Foundation, and later from the Ford Foundation, Dr. Shapiro said, "We were able to hire street workers who came from the same neighborhoods as the students at Hughes. Aside from being well versed in drugs, these were aggressive young people. Most of them were in their twenties, and when street gangs had been primarily 'bopping' gangs a few years before, many of the street workers had been war counselors. They had widely diverse educational backgrounds, with one of them having been in college.

"Walking the halls of the high school," Dr. Shapiro told me, "the street workers had no difficulty recognizing who the pushers were. Well, there was a problem once—they frisked somebody who turned out to be a plain-clothes detective from the narcotics squad. Anyway, when they grabbed a pusher, they would bring him to a room in the school set aside for street workers. After that confrontation, the pusher, in most cases, did not return to Hughes. Our operation became such a concern to the pushers that a couple of our people were shot at. But the street workers weren't in the least intimidated. Furthermore, through an assistant to the mayor, I was able to get them policelike badges that said 'Narcotics Control, District 3, Board of Education,' and each worker had a letter from the police commissioner saying he was permitted to wear the badge and to act, in a sense, as a deputy.

"We weren't able to do much," Dr. Shapiro continued, "with kids in the school who were already far gone on drugs, but word was passed around Harlem, where many of our students came from, that Hughes no longer was a 'party school.' Accordingly, incoming classes to Hughes were relatively drug-free while the street worker program was in operation.

"The street workers wanted to make what they were doing into a professional career, and we tried to work out a degree program for them at Hunter College, but it involved such wide variations from traditional academic requirements that it fell through. It's too bad, because a job ladder *could* be developed from street worker to guidance counselor and social worker. Anyway, we developed a strong loyalty to one another, the street workers and I, and the best compliment I have ever received came from a street worker who told the then dean of education at Hunter, 'We want to make this a profession because as of now, the only street worker who is also accepted as a professional is Dr. Shapiro.' "

Elliott Shapiro's responsibility for the street workers' program ended when the city's high schools were suddenly removed from the supervision of the local districts and put under the control of the city-wide Board of Education staff. "After the switch took place, it was a month," Dr. Shapiro remembered ruefully, "before I was offhandedly told that the high schools had been taken away. We had been working with the street workers that whole month. The program lasted awhile longer, but eventually it collapsed because the funding stopped. The foundations had expected the central Board of Education to finance the project once it had been firmly established, but the board didn't consider it a priority. We did prove, however, that it *is* possible to physically protect a school against widespread introduction of drugs. As, by the way, we had been able to protect, at least temporarily, part of a neighborhood on the Lower East Side. We alerted the parents of the children at a school nearby that we were going to try to protect the neighborhood from drugs. It could be dangerous, we told them, but we hoped they would pass along any information to us, however indirectly. Some parents did help, we gave that information to the police, and the pushers were ousted from an apartment in the La Guardia houses that they had used as a base.

"That was another place," Dr. Shapiro said, "we could have used a permanent force of street workers. I still haven't given up the possibility of making street work of that kind a profession. It's only one of a number of ways in which young people, while in high school, could develop community-related skills leading to paraprofessional and then professional careers. Energetic youngsters, for another example, could become involved in checking on housing violations in the neighborhood and seeing that something is done about them. This kind of real work for youngsters still in school is also a way in which their liveliness can be nurtured so that they don't cop out and fall apart. After all, if a child is going to become an independent, reasonably creative adult, he requires an educational environment in which he feels he can make an impact on the real world."

One difficulty with this approach to encouraging the liveliness of public school students is that many teachers and supervisors lack both the conviction and the temperament to accept, let alone act on, Dr. Shapiro's definition of community-related accountability. While he was still community superintendent of District 2, however, Dr. Shapiro did make persistent efforts to break what he calls "the circle of passivity" in which teachers and supervisors, from his point of view, are unduly self-limited.

He had some successes, most notably a remarkable turnout of parents, other community people, and teachers for a November 1971 demonstration at City Hall Park against a particularly damaging act of budget-cutting by the Board of Education. "We had an impact," Dr. Shapiro recalled. "The cutting that finally took place was much less severe. It was an important learning experience, or it should have been. We showed that it *is* possible to unite everyone concerned with education in a given community to act for specific goals. There were five thousand people there from District 2. Can you imagine what the impact would have been if there had also been five thousand people from each of the other thirty-one districts? Over 150,000 people! It would have been the biggest demonstration for children in municipal history. And the board wouldn't have dared cut the budget at all.

"If only we could have had a city-wide demonstration with that many people when the early-childhood program was killed toward the end of my tenure at District 2. The program, which had been pushed by the teachers' union at the bargaining table, was for children as young as four in thoroughly integrated classes, and that included integration across income levels. You see, teachers' children were also part of it. At the time the program started, there was a teacher shortage and the union felt this was a way to persuade former teachers who now had very young children to come back into the system. However, when the board decided to cut early childhood out of the budget, the union felt it had more pressing priorities to bargain for, and out went early childhood. That program changed the lives of many children and their parents. I remember a woman telling me, 'You know, I used to hit the children, but now I know there's another way.' "

I remembered, as I told Dr. Shapiro, what a black mother had said to me one afternoon about the early-childhood program while she had been waiting to see Dr. Shapiro in his community superintendent's office. "I have one child in the first grade, another in the second grade," she told me, "and one in the pre-kindergarten program. The youngest one already knows more than his older brother and sister. At least, let me have for this child what the others didn't get."

"Yes, I know the mother you mean," Dr. Shapiro said. "The board cut early childhood out of the budget because it was expensive. And it was—about three thousand dollars for each child. *But what is there more valuable to spend money on?* And in any case, it will ultimately be more expensive to society *not* to have such programs."

In Dr. Shapiro's office at Yeshiva, I asked him why it has not become commonplace for teachers and supervisors to ally themselves with parents to save such programs as the early-childhood one—all the more so these days when funds for all kinds of school programs are being cut throughout the country.

"To answer that," he said, "we have to go back to 'the circle of passivity.' Think of the training of a middle-class child who succeeds in school according to the school's criteria of success. As John Holt and others have pointed out, it's the kind of training that, by and large, guarantees passivity. If you're too spontaneous or too rebellious in school, you don't succeed. When those who do succeed become teachers or supervisors or, for that matter, voting citizens, they have learned to be quite passive people. And as such, teachers transmit the values with which they were brought up. Therefore it becomes very difficult to enliven them. I would say that my greatest disappointment through these years has been teacher passivity.

"I used to say, and I still believe," Shapiro continued, "that if teachers were to organize into a strong union that would protect them from being fired except for real cause, they could become lively in the sense of engaging themselves in working for the needs of the community and the needs of the school itself. A powerful union, such as the United Federation of Teachers has become in New York City, and through merger throughout the state, should serve to allow teachers to nurture their own independence. But that hasn't happened yet. It's that passivity again.

"When I worked in District 2," Dr. Shapiro said, "I met frequently with the union's district representative and its borough representative, as well as with teachers. There were some faculty people who were very impressive and had the potential to become exceptionally good teachers. But when they boasted about their output into the neighborhoods near their schools, I had to point out to them that it was really very small compared with the output from my office, which was separated by miles from some of those neighborhoods. And I used to say to all the teachers that it's not enough for them to proclaim, 'Teachers Want What Children Need,' only when it's time to negotiate a new contract. Throughout the school year, teachers have to *show* they really believe that.

"I also used to meet with all the principals in the district. I tried to make them realize the strength *they* could have if they developed honest ties with teachers and parents on goals that would be mutually rewarding. I don't think I had much effect. A few of the principals would get up and say, 'We as educators can't take on all the ills of society.' And others would tell stories of the dangers principals face if they take a firm stand in a community where different factions are trying to use the schools to establish a power base."

Dr. Shapiro had had some experience on that kind of firing line. While he had been principal of P.S. 119 in Harlem, a local self-styled militant whose initial aim appeared to be all-black control of Harlem schools began a campaign to have Shapiro thrown out by P.S. 119's parent body. The militant was told by representatives of the parents' association that they would welcome him if he cared to come up to the second floor of the school and then they would be delighted to throw him out the window. Dr. Shapiro wondered at the time why they had chosen the second floor, since P.S. 119 had three stories. He finally concluded it was an act of compassion.

"I told that story to the principals in District 2," Dr. Shapiro said, "but it didn't seem to reassure them. A few, however, have learned how to be strong in alliance with parents, even in those districts where, in the name of community control, small groups of people threaten bodily harm to those they oppose and wait in a bloc at school board meetings until midnight, when most of the parents have gone home, to bring up an important issue."

Dr. Shapiro regrets, in retrospect, that he tried to work with the principals as a group. "That was a fundamental mistake," he told me soon after his retirement as community superintendent. "I should have worked with them one by one, on a counseling basis, without telling them we were engaged in counseling. On the other hand, I should also have concentrated on those few who were making some movement toward real leadership. On the third hand, I was involved in so many daily crises, including continual battles against budget cuts, that I didn't have the time to do either. Anyway, I was more a failure than a success in enlivening the principals of District 2."

During that conversation, which had as a vigorous obbligato the shouts of children from the playground below his apartment, the retired community superintendent told of his expectations once he had decided to teach at Yeshiva. "I have some hope in the students I'll be working with. Most will wind up in positions of leadership in the schools, and the majority, I am glad to hear, plan to stay in this city, or work in some other large city. It may be that with them, I can finally start to find out how to really enliven people working in education."

At Yeshiva, Dr. Shapiro, among other assignments, is in charge of an internship program for administrators. "Some," he explained, "work in schools, including one or two private schools, and a few are interns in college administration. I ask them to keep a log of what they're doing, including their justifications, or lack of them, for what they're doing. I also ask them to explore what may be behind the scenes in the politics of whatever educational situation they're working in. And I ask them about the decision-making opportunities they have in the course of their work, and how they react to those opportunities. Is there any risk-taking in what they finally decide to do? To what extent do they encourage others to take risks?"

In addition to the internship program, Dr. Shapiro is one of three advisers in a doctoral seminar in education. His office being as open as those he had at P.S. 119 and during his terms as community superintendent, Dr. Shapiro also acts as informal adviser to a number of students who just walk in. At Yeshiva he also teaches a course in the politics of education, as well as a series of seminarlike sessions on educational leadership.

I wondered how he had adjusted to a less demanding schedule than the fourteen hours a day (except for Sunday, when he sometimes worked twelve hours) he had become accustomed to as a community superintendent in the public school system.

"It's been no problem." He smiled. "I'm able to read a lot more than I used to, especially books by people who have been thinking very hard about how to make education a humanitarian enterprise that works through a democratic process. Unfortunately, they themselves haven't had sufficient direct experience in schools. So I enjoy those books in a critical sort of way. I'm still learning, and that keeps me kind of young. The way I feel about getting off the fourteen-hour-a-day treadmill reminds me of something Paul Goodman used to say. If you're sixty-five, and you enter a marathon race, nobody expects you to win. It's enough just to finish. So while running, you can stop and wander in the fields and see things nobody else sees and hear things nobody else hears and have experiences nobody else has. Before, when I was a superintendent, I was expected to win."

"Did you?" I asked.

"In education," he said, "if you don't lose disastrously, you kind of win."

I asked him how successful he has been in enlivening his present students on their way to positions as principals and superintendents and other kinds of school administrators throughout the country.

"It takes time," Dr. Shapiro answered. "What I'm trying to do right now is to get them to explore themselves. As an assignment for the class this afternoon, for instance, I asked them to think about the motivations they have for going into education. And how much pressure they think they'll be able to stand. And what their reactions will be to conflicting pressures. It's a livelier group than most. I am troubled, though, by the fact that they tend not to be readers. To them history began when their own personal history began. Would you believe that most of them didn't know that the *Atlantic Monthly* is a magazine? But then teachers never were very well educated. However, these youngsters, having grown up in the era of what they call 'rap sessions,' are very good discussants. I sometimes think they don't read much because you can't have a rap session with a book.

"What I'm especially concerned with in the students I deal with," Dr. Shapiro continued, "is not only the competencies they develop, but also how they use them. They can become experts in educational change, but what *kind* of expert? One route is to become a soft-sell manipulator of others rather than someone committed to a humanitarian ideal and willing to actually participate with others in a truly transactional relationship. You see, if they don't remain faithful to an ideal of some kind, they're going to sell out without even knowing they're doing it."

Dr. Shapiro still had a few telephone calls to make, and I went up to a spacious room on the seventeenth floor of Yeshiva with a striking view of lower Manhattan to the Brooklyn Bridge and beyond. Two students were already seated at one end of a large round table in the center of the room. They were discussing a paper one of them was about to hand in to Dr. Shapiro.

"Oh, *yeah!*" the other one commented. "He loves that. 'If you wish to have a humanitarian school, it is possible to use humanitarian techniques to get there.' That's it."

Agreed on the likely impact of the paper, the two began to discuss their jobs. "I'm going to leave," the writer of the paper said. "There's too much political crap working as an administrator in that school district."

"That's the name of the game," his friend answered. "You've got to learn the ropes."

"Maybe so," the other student said, "but once I get my doctorate, I'm leaving this city, all five boroughs of it. I'm going to look around Westchester or maybe Connecticut."

"Yup," his friend said. "Once you've got that doctorate, you really have a meal ticket."

Gradually more students came in until seventeen, six of them women, were sitting around the table. Dr. Shapiro arrived carrying two brief cases and a file folder under his arm. Several students went over to him and, a pencil in his mouth, he thumbed through his appointment book to find space for appointments with them.

"All right," Dr. Shapiro started the discussion. "Why are you going into administrative work? Why do you want to be a principal or an assistant principal? How committed are you to the humanistic rhetoric we mouth? Do you really have a desire to take on the responsibility of change? I know that we're becoming expert in developing the language of educational change, but I don't know how willing you are to begin the *process* of change and to see it all the way through—even if it's a lot easier not to. *How willing are you to move against power?"*

One student said it was hard for him to answer that question until he was actually confronted with the problem. "What you did to get a new school in Harlem, the ad in the paper and all the rest of it," he said to Dr. Shapiro, "must have taken a lot of guts. I think I could do something like that, but I won't know until I have to."

"First of all," Dr. Shapiro began, "it wouldn't have happened if there hadn't been a strong parents' association, and that took a number of years to build because I had to prove to those parents that I really cared about their children. When we were ready to move, I knew I was taking a risk, but I had prepared a lot of countervailing power if we needed it. We had developed all kinds of background support. We had contacted any number of unions before we put that ad in the paper. The fish workers' union, the automobile workers' union, the textile workers' union, the pulp and paper and sulfite workers. They supported us with letters and telegrams and they would have joined us in a mass demonstration if we had needed them. This took place at a time, by the way, when the United Federation of Teachers had *maybe* twelve hundred members. The U.F.T., so we heard from some of its members afterward, learned a lot from us in that campaign. Anyway, you have to develop expertise in building countervailing power if you're going into battle with a school system."

"Yeah," a short, intense young man said. "When you start to fight an institution, you can't do it with rubber bands because it's going to fight back with rocks and heavy ammunition."

Another participant in the class, a teacher, told of several decisions he had already had to make as to whether to take risks or not. In different ways, each decision had been a compromise.

"We all compromise," Dr. Shapiro said, "all the time. But do we wind up corrupt nice guys who have eventually forgotten what it is not to compromise?"

"I know what you mean," a student said. "While I was in administration, I saw so many people in that office who were servicing nobody but themselves. And I saw myself getting to be like those disgusting creatures, so now I'm a reading teacher, on a clinical basis, going to various schools and working with children, not with administrators. It may look like a step backward, but when the final results are in, it may turn out to have been a powerful first step in learning how to be of real use to children."

Dr. Shapiro nodded in agreement, but another student mildly disagreed. "To bring about change," he said, "you have to go *as high as you can* in the system because there's no way to change the inside from outside the system. And you *can* go high up without selling out."

A discussion followed on how well teacher-training institutions prepare new teachers for real-life classrooms.

"Do you notice how we speak of teacher-*training* institutions?" Dr. Shapiro said. "You don't hear the term *doctor-training* institutions. If you use the word *training,* it's as if you're dealing with people as though they're animals who have to be taught to obey."

With regard to how professors of education are preparing their students for a first year of teaching, Dr. Shapiro emphasized that "they actually prepare aspiring teachers for their second year or their third year, but not for the first year. Very often, beginning teachers who have the best motivations for wanting to work with children are disasters in their first year. Because they like the kids, they try to create free interplay between themselves and the kids. At that point the kids don't know whether this teacher is an adult or another child. A teacher has to recognize that he *is* an adult and that children require from an adult, before anything else, the sense that they are safe in the environment the adult is setting. In the first year, a teacher has to develop a constitution, as it were, or a body of law within the classroom that he applies consistently. If you do that, if you can become an efficient adult in a classroom, you can go on to experiment to your heart's content.

"But what happens is that many new teachers do not act consistently in their relations with the children. They so want the children to have a feeling of success that they violate their own regulations without being aware of it. But the children know, and they decide that the teacher doesn't mean what he says. Then, if a class is getting more and more 'difficult,' the new teacher may become authoritarian because that seems to him the only way to get order in the classroom. That's the pivotal seductive moment for a teacher. Will he go on being authoritarian or will he remember why he went into teaching in the first place?"

Toward the end of the class, Dr. Shapiro posed a question to the students. "With all the current emphasis on reading scores," he said, "what do you do if you're being pressured by the principal, who is in turn being pressured by the community superintendent, to get those scores up? One way of doing it is teaching to the test."

"Yeah, I know about that," said a long-haired student with a Pancho Villa mustache. "One year I coached the kids so hard I damn near *gave* them the test before the big day came. They failed anyway. No more. *Now* I just teach reading, for real. But a lot of teachers are still into coaching the kids in order to prove that *they* know how to teach. They're not doing it to improve the kids' reading."

"All right," Dr. Shapiro said, "let me change that question. Think about this for the next session. Make believe that you're principal of an elementary school in a poor neighborhood. The reading scores are quite low, and you are going to be held accountable for whether or not the children's reading improves —the measure being how they do on the standardized reading tests. If the reading scores don't improve, there's a very good chance you'll be ousted. You yourself believe, however, that teaching to the test does not really improve reading, even if the scores indicate that it has. What do you do in this situation? In the few minutes left, we can start on this if you like."

"I would teach to the test," a student said, "and I probably would falsify the scores if I had to."

"Believe me," interrupted another student, who has worked on a State Department of Education team evaluating various school programs in the city, "there's a lot of tampering with the scores going on. More and more each year."

"But by doing that or by teaching to the test," the first student insisted, "I'd have the time to try different experimental techniques until the children's reading genuinely improved. In the meantime I'd show the local board what they want to see."

A half dozen of the other students nodded in agreement.

"No," a young woman broke in. "I'd try to work with the parents to convince them that the scores are not all that important. I'd tell them exactly what we were doing—let's say, starting open classroom situations—and I'd also tell them that in two years the scores will go up and they'll be honest scores."

"Remember," Dr. Shapiro said, "this school is in a poor neighborhood. Would the parents buy that? And if the scores don't go up in two years, what are you going to do then?"

The young woman did not have a ready answer.

In the corridor, as we were walking to the elevator, I asked Dr. Shapiro how he would handle the dilemma he had given his class. "I wouldn't go along with teaching to the test. We didn't do that at 119, and I wouldn't do it now. I would go to the parents. Not all of them at first. I'd go to those parents who are most likely to understand that test scores are not always a true indicator of lasting progress. In fact, as I would show them, there is research indicating that kids who have been coached for reading tests lose most of their apparent 'gains' in a short time. I'd explain to those parents what we're actually doing about reading and what our realistic expectations are. And then I'd ask them to carry the ball for us with the other parents."

When we were back in his office, I asked Dr. Shapiro how his wife was. Shortly before he retired from the public school system, there had been a party for Dr. Shapiro in the gym of P.S. 116, the school in which he had his office. There, in between the spirited Latin jazz of a junior high school band in the district —a band made visually distinctive by a girl with a floppy red hat attacking the piano while teachers did the boogaloo—there was a brief ceremony. Standing with his arm around his wife, Florence, Dr. Shapiro had said, "If I have been able to accomplish anything, it was not only because of the dedicated help of people in Harlem and in this district, but also because there was always one person who would not allow me to have anxiety over the consequences to my job of doing what I felt had to be done. It was this lady, Mrs. Shapiro."

"A lot of people"—Mrs. Shapiro, a short, slight woman, had taken the microphone—"have asked me to try to convince him to stay. Frankly, I don't want to because I think he has earned the right to relax a little and think a little and do some of the things he has wanted to do for some time. He wants to write, and I have bought him a typewriter. But I think you know that whatever he does will benefit people."

Two years later, both Shapiros were still working. His wife, Dr. Shapiro told me, was teaching English as a second language two days a week at a parochial school on the Lower East Side. "They're very poor children," Dr. Shapiro added, "as poor as these." He pointed to several photographs on the wall over his desk of black children busily engaged in what looked to be various corners of an open classroom.

The photographs had been taken by the children's teacher, Ellen Shapiro. A year before, Dr. Shapiro had told me proudly of his daughter's work in a Harlem school. "She's a superior teacher," he had said. "She does get discouraged now and then because there are problems. One of the teachers she works with, for instance, insists on using the television set. Everybody sits and watches because it's an educational program, but that teacher doesn't realize that the children have been passive all that time. Ellen, however, is getting less and less discouraged. She'll go on."

So she had. "In a year," Dr. Shapiro said, looking at the photographs, "Ellen has become an outstanding kindergarten teacher. She has gained experience in learning how to organize the kinds of spatial relationships that make it possible for a number of creative activities to be going on at the same time in a classroom without chaos resulting. She's in another Harlem school. It's half black and half Puerto Rican. I observed her teaching last year and again this term, and she's far better than she was when she started. Ellen has more than survived."

Picking up one of his brief cases as he told me about his daughter, Dr. Shapiro started to stuff some papers into it, but was interrupted by another phone call from one of his students. When he had finished, I asked him why he is listed as a visiting professor at Yeshiva.

"When I started here," he said, "I was offered the job title of professor, period, but I wasn't all that sure about what I wanted to do. That's how I came to be a visiting professor. I'm not sure where I'm visiting from. Maybe"—he laughed—"from the real world. Anyway, as it has worked out, I am a voting member of the faculty and I'm also a member of the welfare committee that deals with salaries and working conditions."

It was getting late, and as we left his office, I asked Dr. Shapiro how he assessed the impact he had made after some four decades in public education.

"Well," he said, pushing his eyeglasses farther back on his head, "going back to the elementary school in Harlem, I think that our battle with the Board of Education showed everyone that it was possible to do battle with a central authority and to do battle successfully. I think that realization would have occurred in any case, but we speeded it up a little. So that was useful."

"Tell me," I asked, "was there really a rat in sight on the day that the mayor visited the school? One of the city officials who was with the major that day told me that he *heard* the kids shouting, 'Rat! Rat! There goes the rat!' but there was no such animal in sight."

Dr. Shapiro smiled. "Actually, there was one. Maybe it's too bad the rat showed up that morning. You see, if we had not gotten a response to our demand for a new school, we would have had thousands and thousands of people out to demonstrate the following Monday. The teachers and parents had worked so hard organizing the demonstration that they even had commitments from their relatives to attend. Maybe, if there had been such a huge demonstration at that time, it would have been more of a contribution to the learning process than the emergence of the famous rat.

"You asked about what impact I might have made through the years. Now what else?" He paused for a while. "I think I left something of myself where I worked as community superintendent. The parents there are still fighting the central Board of Education, questioning its edicts, and coming down in force to meetings of the board. Sometimes they even win. Also, there must have been some seven hundred teachers in the classes I taught for five or six years in the 1960s at City College. A number of them, I think, were influenced by me, along with some of the teachers I have worked with as a principal and as a community superintendent.

"Going back to P.S. 119 in Harlem," Dr. Shapiro said, "I think we had something to do, at an early point, with the breakthrough of black teachers into jobs as principals and assistant principals in the system. By around 1967 or so, the *majority* of black teachers in supervisory positions throughout the whole city had come from P.S. 119. We were so far ahead of the others.

"As for the children of P.S. 119," Dr. Shapiro continued, "I don't know exactly what influence I had on them. I did hear that when our children went on to junior high school, they weren't as angry as the other children but they were more specifically assertive in their own behalf than the other kids. A principal told me, 'I always know a P.S. 119 child by the directness of his relationship with adults and by the fact that he doesn't immediately make us the enemy.' "

There was another pause. "But I have a feeling," Dr. Shapiro

said softly, "that an awful lot of the boys from 119 are dead by
now."

"Do you mean literally dead?" I asked.

"Yes. From dope. A while ago, I saw a boy of about sixteen
in a supermarket. He was mopping the floors. The boy came up
to me and said, 'Aren't you Dr. Shapiro from 119?' I recognized
him. I didn't remember his last name, but I knew his first name.
I asked him how his brother was. 'He's dead,' the boy told me.
Looking at him, I had the sense that he was overcoming a drug
habit of his own. There are soft signs you can detect. I wondered
whether he was on methadone. Afterward, thinking about our
meeting, I was pleased at first that he had a job. But then I
asked myself where he could move to from that job. A promotion to the checkout counter?

"Yet there have been some successes, sometimes depending
on the limitations of your definition of success. I've met former
students from P.S. 119 who have responsible jobs. One is working in a department store, another is a bank teller, and some
are teachers. And just the other day, I met a young woman
who's involved in pre-med studies.

"But dope"—he shook his head—"killed some of the rest of
them. When I was visiting a high school as District 2 superintendent, I saw a large number of P.S. 119 kids. One was about
finished because of heroin. Soon after, I visited P.S. 92, the new
school that took the place of 119. There was that same boy,
nodding, in the playground." Dr. Shapiro sighed. "As I said,
there have been some successes among our former students at
P.S. 119. But on the whole, I would say we probably had more
failures than we had successes."

"Wouldn't there have been more failures if you hadn't been
there?" I asked.

"I hope so," Dr. Shapiro said, "but I can't tell for sure. However, these days, when protests are made at Board of Education
meetings, there's usually a strong representation from our old
Harlem school in the new building. So that spirit is still there.

"It's hard, though, to say what influences you have had. After you're gone, maybe almost nothing is left unless you've made a seminal discovery like Newton or Einstein. Anyway, I'm not done yet, although the odds may be ten to one that I'll be successful from now on as a teacher of teachers and supervisors. I'm not depressed, you see. I'm just trying to be realistic.

"There are little things over the decades that have happened for the good because of my, let us say, intervention. But they have to be nurtured because they're hothouse plants that are likely to die when they're exposed to the weather. I guess I may be due some credit for providing the soil in which those plants can grow. And if I have left, in a few places, the spirit that does encourage others to nurture them, I will have been, in a small way, successful."

Epilogue

Miguel Piñero is an ex-junkie and an alumnus of Sing Sing. He is also exceptionally intelligent and has found his true calling as a playwright—one of his plays, *Short Eyes*, about prison life, having won overwhelming critical approval. However, during all his years in the schools of New York City, Piñero was categorized as dumb and disruptive.

"That school time," he has told me, "is all a blur. I don't remember the names of any of the teachers I had. And they certainly didn't know or care who the hell I was. I learned to read by myself, you know. Comic books. Now I see kids like I was. A lot of kids. A lot of dead souls. And just like in my time, nobody gives a damn about what happens to them."

Piñero spent much of his school time on the Lower East Side of Manhattan. It's called District 1 by the Board of Education. "Our district," says a young Puerto Rican woman there, "has a 50 percent dropout rate before high school age. Seventy-five percent of the kids read below grade level. Now where do you think they're going to wind up?"

In another part of the city, the Fortune Society, an organization of ex-convicts, has started its own teaching program so that those of its members whom the public schools would not educate can at least achieve enough literacy to apply for a job and to finally recognize that they are not irredeemably dumb. One of the students, who is twenty-one, went through twelve years in the public school system and did not know the alphabet when he came out.

In Watertown, Connecticut, Lance Odden, headmaster of the Taft School, explains the rise in applications to his and other private secondary schools around the country: "If nothing else, we can guarantee that anyone who graduates will be able to read and write."

But of course, those of the young who are poor and in the public schools cannot transfer to the Taft School. And many of them will leave the public school system, with or without a diploma, only minimally able to read and write. Yet they were not born dumb. Their burden is that they have not been successfully taught. And that happens, says Dr. Kenneth Clark, the only black member of the New York State Board of Regents, "because they are not respected as human beings—they are regarded as subhumans, as non-educable. They are expected to fail."

Most teachers, of course, would deny Dr. Clark's accusation, would deny they see these kids as subhuman. But what *are* their expectations of them? A teacher in a New York City ghetto school said in January 1976: "Just last night when I was marking some reading tests, I realized how much I've really given up on these kids—not consciously, of course, but unconsciously. I was thinking how bright these kids were—and then I realized they were reading on a fifth-grade level and they were fifteen years old."

This teacher will not, of course, be penalized for her low expectations, conscious or unconscious, of her students. Nor will she or her school be admonished by the public school system's hierarchy for the destructive results of those low expectations. Actually, as Kenneth Clark says, "The city's teachers have been consistently rewarded financially for their failure to deliver needed services to lower status children." Not only in New York, but in nearly every city in the country.

On the other hand, in East Palo Alto, California, a small private institution—Nairobi Schools (founded in 1969)—guarantees to teach black children to read within one school year or it will refund the tuition payments. (Tuition varies according to family income; and as of June 1975, according to *The New York Times,* twenty-eight of the thirty-five families involved were receiving financial assistance.)

In the history of the school so far, all of its low-income black students have learned to read, along with other essential skills. Until the Nairobi School came into being, says its founder, Gertrude Wilks, "our children were moving out of the eighth grade, illiterate, into the mortification process of an unteaching public high school. . . . What our children get *here* is self-confidence and self-esteem. It is a crucial attitude in early childhood."

Mrs. Wilks has strong empirical knowledge of the value of the self-esteem that can come from learning that one can learn. As Sandra Blakeslee reported in the *Times:* "When her oldest son graduated from an East Palo Alto high school in the early 1960's, he could not read well enough to get a job. Today he is in prison. Mrs. Wilks was able to help her second son in time. He has a master's degree in political science from Harvard University."

The graduates of the Nairobi School have had no difficulty enrolling in colleges and universities throughout the country. Why has this school not failed its children? Because its teachers must teach successfully in order to keep their jobs. Previously, before the school was founded, Mrs. Wilks points out, "I saw that white teachers were afraid of our black children. And they figured that black parents don't care about their children. But I knew that black parents did care about their children. Teacher attitudes, in my view, were blocking the door."

And in many public schools, teacher attitudes keep on blocking the door. Also in the way, in not a few cases, is a decided lack of competency. Clearly, as Harvey Scribner has pointed out, it makes no educational sense to grant a teacher the equivalent of lifelong tenure once he or she has survived the probationary period. Rather than being permanent or quasipermanent, licenses should be renewable, following an exploration of how well a teacher's students have been learning—and what the explanations are for those children who have *not* been learning.

Sometimes a pattern of teacher failure is quite clear. In a Massachusetts city, for instance, for five years children had been moving into a fifth-grade math class with reasonable skills in the subject gained from their previous teachers. (Some of the kids were better than others, but nearly all were where they should have been in math.) And for five years, most of the children who came *out* of that fifth-grade class showed marked deterioration in math. Manifestly, this was a teacher in charge of the wrong subject, and perhaps a teacher who should not have been teaching at all.

This kind of pattern is not uncommon, but other forms of teacher deficiency are not so easily italicized. Yet after many hours of observing in classrooms, I am convinced that a fair determination of teacher competency—*and* teacher attitude toward what Kenneth Clark calls "lower status" children—is not all that difficult to make. It obviously can't be done on the basis of a single visit; but a series of sizable visits spread over some months, together with an examination of each child's previous school history and present *capacities,* can lead to an equitable assessment. And when grave evidence of probable teacher failure is found, the teacher in question should be brought up on charges, with all due process protections (including his or her own counsel).

But more than the individual teacher is at issue. Often whole schools are at grievous fault. As has been shown in this book, there is no reason why "uneducables" cannot be enabled to learn—whether in Martin Schor's elementary school, John Simon's public school classes in a church basement, or the junior high school of which Luther Seabrook was principal until he became, for a time, community superintendent of the schools in Harlem until he was forced out because he wouldn't play the old patronage politics with the local school board. (Decentralization is no guarantee of learning either.) Therefore, if, for one example, a school is not succeeding in teaching its students to read at least at grade level, the failing leadership of that school should be held accountable—with principals and other administrators being brought up on charges of incompetency.

But who is to be involved in deciding and evaluating criteria of competency? Outside professional educators, to be sure. That is, people who not only are not part of the faculty of the particular school, but also are not employed by the particular public school system. And also, there should be parent involvement— parents and their children, as Harvey Scribner keeps emphasizing, being the consumers of public education.

However, as Scribner and Leonard Stevens, his former special assistant in New York, point out in the September 1974 issue of the educational journal *Phi Delta Kappa:*

> Teachers often argue that they are professionals as much as doctors and lawyers and therefore they should have comparable professional power to regulate and control their own ranks. This argument, however, selectively ignores two central factors: 1) teachers are public employees, and 2) their clients are in the classroom by law and not by voluntary choice. These are more than incidental points; indeed, they constitute powerful arguments for greater . . . parent participation in the planning and operation of teacher competency systems.

And, I would add, for greater parent participation in setting up and monitoring competency systems by which to evaluate principals and other administrators.

The problem with the Scribner-Stevens approach, however, is how this degree and durability of parent participation is to be organized and implemented, as against increasingly well-organized teachers and administrators. As Dr. John Merrow II of the Institute for Educational Leadership in Washington observes concerning the parent constituency in public education:

> In a sense, everybody supports the schools; in another sense, nobody does. We all believe in public education, if not for our own children, then for everybody else's. But there is no organized lobby group with the clout of, say, doctors, railroads, or even conservationists. There are groups like the Public Education Association in New York, the National Committee for Citizens in Education, and the Institute for Responsive Education, but those organizations are generally short on resources, public identity, and political influence.

If there is to be an effective organized lobby with the intent of making schools accountable for their failures, many parents will have to reeducate themselves. In *Make Your Schools Work,* Harvey Scribner and Leonard Stevens emphasize:

> Parents have been trained that it is not their place to question educational practice, that it is inappropriate for them to be critical and discontented. The role of the good parent is part of the legend: to be supportive, to be helpful, to rally other taxpayers in support of schools, to belong to the P.T.A., to make sure the young stay in school, to come to graduation ceremonies. Parents have yet to take their ultimate role, their ultimate responsibility: to control their schools as a piece of their government. The day will come, we hope, in some communities, small and large, when parents will say to the professionals they employ, "This is what we want for our children. Don't tell us the reasons it can't be done. Tell us how to do it. Or give us a better idea."

The notion of large-scale parent involvement of this nature in the schools appalls many professional educators. Albert Shanker, president of the American Federation of Teachers, warns that "When you encourage large groups of citizens to participate, then the whole function of education can no longer proceed, just as a hospital couldn't function if everyone in the community decided to come in and participate, to advise the doctors and the nurses as to what to do. Now, there are in each field professionals who have some understanding of what ought be done and to some extent they have to be isolated so that they can do their work. So it is in education."

Yet it is precisely these isolated professionals who have blighted the lives of many of their students—especially "lower-status" youngsters. And while there are a number of cases moving through the courts that may eventually lead to the possibility of widespread educational malpractice suits, no such substantive legal doctrine yet exists to give educators meaningful pause. Accordingly, education professionals—unlike doctors—are isolated to the point of nearly absolute protection from the consequences of any harm they do.

As Scribner and Stevens have indicated, moreover, these professionals are *public* employees engaged in a responsibility of the most fundamental concern to parents. The greater participation of parents in making educators accountable for the fulfillment of that responsibility is not going to mean hordes of disruptive adults swarming daily through the schools. Not only do most parents have neither the time nor the inclination for such swarming, but parents also do recognize that it is destructive, to say the least, for professionals to be continually interrupted, let alone harassed, while exercising their skills. A parent who wants his child to be taught well is not going to get in the way of the teaching.

The increased involvement of parents in the schools—if it happens—will focus on the *results* of the teaching and on the quality of the supervision of the teaching by administrators. If those results are failing, then, I would hope, parents will indeed participate in evaluating the competence of the professionals responsible for those results.

In some respects, of course, this concept of making public education *public* is not new. In a sizable number of middle-class and upper-middle-class communities around the country, parents have always insisted that their schools measure up to the potential of their children. Even at these income levels, however, not nearly enough parents have been as active as they could and should have been to remind those who work in the schools that they are employed by the citizens who send their children there.

It is in working-class and poor neighborhoods, with some exceptions, that the voices of parents are hardly heard at all, even though their schools are most in need of a reexamination of the qualifications and attitudes of those who work in them. In New York City, for instance, where reading scores—as nearly everywhere else—are directly related to the income levels of the neighborhoods in which the schools are located, it has been possible for years to be graduated from a non-specialized city high school with the ability to read at only an eighth-grade level. Each year thousands of children in working-class and poor neighborhoods are *that* badly scarred by their public school system as they graduate into limbo. But there have been few organized protests by these youngsters' parents. They have indeed followed Albert Shanker's advice and have allowed the education professionals to operate—on their children—in isolation.

A few years ago, I took part in a three-day symposium in New York City on school reform. Those involved, including parents, had come from all over the country, and the assemblage was unabashedly pluralistic as to race, income level, and educational philosophy. A bountiful offering of ideas—educational vouchers, startlingly multi-dimensional ways of planning learning space, resplendent new curricula—were explored and debated. But the most powerful impact was made on the symposium's last day by Ellen Lurie, a battered veteran of many school wars.

I've known Ellen Lurie from the beginning of my own involvement in the schools. Through the years, she seemed ubiquitous—at Board of Education meetings, at demonstrations, and in the schools themselves, absorbing the kind of precisely detailed information that made her 1970 book, *How to Change the Schools: A Parent's Action Handbook on How to Fight the System,* a model of knowledgeable action for parents in any city in the country. For five years, Ellen had been a member of School Board 6 in upper Manhattan, finally resigning in protest against the powerlessness of the parents of that district against the centralized, serpentinely manipulative Board of Education. She had also been immersed in angry boycotts against the schools called by the Harlem Parents Committee, among other groups; and she was a voluble member of EQUAL, a group that worked to develop support for school integration in white communities. In addition, Ellen had taught at the New School for Social Research as well as having been training director for United Bronx Parents, a remarkably energetic organization aimed at forcefully motivating professional educators to discard their self-fulfilling prophecies.

At that symposium on school reform, after all the pennants for a glorious new world of education had been unfurled, Ellen rose, and began:

I speak as a parent, with five children in the public school system. I've been trying to change the schools for eighteen years, having started, before my first child came, as a community worker in East Harlem, where we were organizing a huge campaign for new schools. From then to now, I have been deluded so many times by ideas and goals that were supposed to be *the* answer to enabling kids to learn. And because I have been deluded so often, I'm very skeptical of all the new answers I've heard here.

For many years, I thought new schools would do it. And so I fought very hard for new schools, and the new schools were as bad as the old schools. Oh, the rooms were beautiful, but the children weren't learning very much. Then, for many years, I worked with—I hate to say it—Albert Shanker. I marched on the first two United Federation of Teachers picket lines because I thought that low teachers' salaries were what was wrong with the schools. So we fought for a teachers' union and for collective bargaining. So now there's a strong union and collective bargaining, and our kids still aren't learning.

Then I looked around my own neighborhood and I was positive that it was because the schools were segregated that everything was wrong. So I worked for integration; but as a school board member, I found that whatever solutions we developed were shot down by the Board of Education, which itself was so inept and insensitive that its impact on our schools and on black-white relationships in our district was just plain destructive.

At this point, one parent in our neighborhood screamed at me, "If you think integration is such a good idea, why don't you send your own children to school in Harlem?" And for two years, I did send my two oldest children—by bus—fifty blocks to Harlem. And they were safe there. But that wasn't the answer either.

Next we decided, "O.K., we'll run our own schools. Community control is the answer." But what we got was an election procedure that guaranteed our non-participation in some of the most crucial areas of real parent input into the schools —no control over most of our budget, no say as to who teaches and who shouldn't teach in our schools. It had happened

again. We grab an idea and say, "Gee, maybe *this* is going to
do it," and it turns out we don't have any real power over
what's going on, whatever happens to the idea.

But I haven't given up. I still believe that we have to and that
we can find alternatives to what exists. I still believe in new
schools. I still believe in well-paid teachers. I still believe in
local control. I still believe in integration, but it has to be real
integration, not abandonment of the kids. Like years back,
when black children were transported into our neighborhood, they were entirely abandoned once they arrived. The
schools to which they were sent received no special services,
and the teachers were given no special training. And so the
black children, having suffered years of educational neglect,
left to learn as best they could, often failed, as the white
children watched and had all their preconceived prejudices
reinforced. That is *not* integration. That *is* a thoughtless,
greatly harmful Board of Education.

So here we are after all those battles. Let me look back for
a moment. In 1953 in this city, before the Supreme Court's
Brown v. *Board of Education* decision, before the teachers
got higher salaries, before we got "compensatory education,"
before a whole lot of things happened that were supposed to
make the schools *work,* a black child in the public school
system was, on the average, reading two years behind the
average white child on the eighth-grade level. And nearly
two decades later, after all the "improvements" in the school
system, the average black kid in the eighth grade is *six years*
behind the average white kid.

And the Hispanic kids are even farther behind. Just last
year, a principal on the West Side of Manhattan was telling
a group of parents, "Well, yes, some of the Puerto Rican
children in my school can't read, but you should know how
innovative they are. Some of them work for messenger ser-

vices and they go out on the street and have some stranger read the address for them on whatever they have to deliver so that they can keep their jobs." This principal was *bragging* about how these kids in the school for which *he* is responsible are able to cope with *not* reading!

So what do we do now? First, we have to keep on working to make our schools *ours*. And second, for us to begin to get the power that will finally make it possible for the schools to be accountable, we must find out what actually goes on in our schools and compare them with other schools. Parents should organize to get this information. Which schools are over-crowded, and which are underutilized? What are the class sizes? What are the real rates of absenteeism, among teachers as well as kids? Which schools in Spanish-speaking neighborhoods have enough truly bilingual teachers? How many teachers in a school actually live in that community? How many teachers and principals are actually involved in the affairs of the community? How many of them visit the parents, and not only when the child is in trouble? How many schools are giving parents and children a choice of learning programs—Montessori, traditional, open classroom? Is there corporal punishment, or the constant threat of corporal punishment, in a school?

Are the children learning? Are they *really* learning? Are they expected by the staff to learn as much and as well as any child in even the most upper-class neighborhood? Or is the expectation level like that of the principal in a Harlem school I visited, where in a third-grade room the children had nothing more to work with than ordinary coloring books. When I asked the principal why they were doing such simple work, he told me, "These children have so many problems at home, we can't add to their difficulties by giving them problems in school too." That principal should not be able to maintain that attitude and remain in that school.

If the reading scores in your school are lower than those in other schools, *why* are they lower? What is being done to raise the scores—and does that have anything to do with raising the actual ability of the children to read? And what about math skills and writing skills and thinking skills?

There is so much more information to be gathered and shared with other parents; and as more parents learn what and who actually get in the way of their children's learning, we will then be able to move to the next stage of power so that, for example, when 70 percent of the children in a school are reading far below grade level, the principal of that school will be removed and will also lose his certificate of competency.

When she finished, there was much cheering of Ellen Lurie, but she herself did not look at all elated. "I didn't say anything revolutionary," she told me. "These are really such modest proposals, considering the stakes involved. But why does it take so long to get any movement at all that makes a dent?"

This has been a book about those, in and outside the schools, who have learned through hard reckoning not to expect any quick transformation of the system. But each has earned his own kind of stubborn hope, if not always optimism, for each knows that *no child* need be "uneducable."

In knowing and having proved that, they are very much in a minority among professional educators—a situation that will persist until there is the kind of accountability throughout the schools that has been so unyieldingly advocated by Ellen Lurie; Harvey Scribner; Elliott Shapiro (now writing rather than teaching because at age sixty-five, despite all he knows, he is too "old" to teach at Yeshiva University); Martin Schor (who reached mandatory retirement age before the very worst, so far, of the budget cuts); John Simon; and Luther Seabrook who, as this book is being completed, has started moving toward his doctorate in education, working with Harvey Scribner at the University of Massachusetts.

While I recognize that, as Ellen Lurie underlines, it will be a long struggle to end the immunity of school professionals who fail to educate, I continue to find it most difficult to understand why it is so hard to at least end the beating of schoolchildren in much of the country. Or does the latter have more than a little to do with the former?

Consider that in America in 1976, a United States district judge in Lubbock, Texas, ruled that an eighteen-year-old boy could not be readmitted to high school until he had subjected himself to paddling by the principal for an unexcused absence. This educational paddling was to be administered with a shaved-off baseball bat. The boy's father pleaded for his son before the court, but he had no standing as compared with the principal.

And so far, the parents of children who are permanently crippled by schools—because those children are made to believe they are dumb—also have no standing against the state. The intent of this book is to leave you with the question of how long, in both cases, this must continue to be.

Index

A Note on the Type

The text of this book was set by computer-driven Cathode Ray Tube in Century Schoolbook, a type face based on Century Expanded, which was designed in 1894 by Linn Boyd Benton (1844–1932). Benton cut Century Expanded in response to Theodore De Vinne's request for an attractive, easy-to-read type face to fit the narrow columns of his *Century Magazine.* Early in the nineteen hundreds Morris Fuller Benton updated and improved Century in several versions for his father's American Type Founders Company. Century remains the only American type face cut before 1910 still widely in use today.

Composed by Datagraphics, Phoenix, Arizona.
Printed and bound by American Book–Stratford Press, Saddle Brook, New Jersey.
Typography and binding design by Virginia Tan.